Management and Visualisation

As organisations of all sizes become increasingly digitalised, a core management challenge remains unresolved. The ability to successfully and sustainably connect the stated vision of an organisation with its strategic plans and, in turn, with the reported reality of day-to-day operations, is largely an elusive ambition, despite the many stated advantages provided by contemporary technologies. In this book, the case is made for visual management as a method of communications, planning, learning and reporting that connects the organisation in a single, meaningful and seamless way.

Throughout this book, visual management is theorised around the position that all forms of management documentation are an artefact of human construction and of the organisation itself that reflects learned patterns of activity. The book places visual management as a more intuitive and seamless method of coordinating, learning and communicating across an organisation than more traditional formats of presenting management documents. Consciously assembling the artefacts of an organisation in order to manage it introduces a layer of criticality that encourages reflection and consistency that is often absent from current management practice. The benefits that a visual approach brings to organisational management are an increasing necessity, as machine learning, robotics and process automation remove traditional roles from organisations and necessitate new views on how individuals now fit into a data-informed business.

The book contributes to the academic debate regarding resource-based and knowledge-based views of the organisation by advocating a different, more holistic viewpoint and will thus appeal to academics and researchers in this area. It would also benefit students across business disciplines, whilst the practical models and tools offered will benefit directors and managers looking to implement their own visual organisational language.

Gordon Fletcher is currently Director of Business 4.0 and the school lead for research at Salford Business School. Gordon has a 25-year record of teaching and professional workshops in the many aspects of the digitalisation of business and society.

Routledge Focus on Business and Management

The fields of business and management have grown exponentially as areas of research and education. This growth presents challenges for readers trying to keep up with the latest important insights. *Routledge Focus on Business and Management* presents small books on big topics and how they intersect with the world of business research.

Individually, each title in the series provides coverage of a key academic topic, whilst collectively, the series forms a comprehensive collection across the business disciplines.

Risk Management Maturity
A Multidimensional Model
Sylwia Bąk and Piotr Jedynak

Neuroscience and Entrepreneurship Research
Researching Brain-Driven Entrepreneurship
Víctor Pérez Centeno

Proposal Writing for Business Research Projects
Peter Samuels

Systems Thinking and Sustainable Healthcare Delivery
Ben Fong

Gender Diversity and Inclusion at Work
Divergent Views from Turkey
Zeynep Özsoy, Mustafa Şenyücel and Beyza Oba

Management and Visualisation
Seeing Beyond the Strategic
Gordon Fletcher

For more information about this series, please visit: www.routledge.com/ Routledge-Focus-on-Business-and-Management/book-series/FBM

Management and Visualisation

Seeing Beyond the Strategic

Gordon Fletcher

Routledge
Taylor & Francis Group

LONDON AND NEW YORK

First published 2023
by Routledge
4 Park Square, Milton Park, Abingdon, Oxon OX14 4RN

and by Routledge
605 Third Avenue, New York, NY 10158

Routledge is an imprint of the Taylor & Francis Group, an informa business

© 2023 Gordon Fletcher

British Library Cataloguing-in-Publication Data
A catalogue record for this book is available from the British Library

ISBN: 978-1-032-30251-5 (hbk)
ISBN: 978-1-032-30252-2 (pbk)
ISBN: 978-1-003-30416-6 (ebk)

DOI: 10.4324/9781003304166

Typeset in Times New Roman
by Apex CoVantage, LLC

Contents

Figures

Tables

The BOOK

1 Introduction

What is visual management?

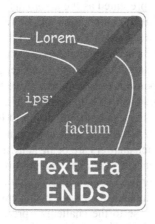

The aftermath of a global pandemic, warfare in Eastern Europe, increasingly uncertain supply chains, spiralling cost of living, populist politics and the consequences of disastrous climate change: all these challenges bring the uncertainty of a hostile world into our most immediate focus. What was once only known through history or television news reporting from a different continent is now – in varying degrees of severity – a daily reality for everyone. Many wits and some more serious reporters even draw upon references and imagery associated with the Four Horsemen of the Apocalypse to punctuate their commentaries (Crabtree 2022; Harris 2022). Such imagery is overly figurative, but the many examples of external threats that can be currently identified confirm the presence of Volatility, Uncertainty, Complexity and Ambiguity (VUCA) throughout our everyday experience (Fletcher and Griffiths 2020). These are ever-present risks to both organisations and individuals (Bennet and Lemoine 2014). The presence of external VUCA in whatever form it assumes distracts from being able to effectively

DOI: 10.4324/9781003304166-1

deal with the multiple smaller and more day-to-day challenges that we need to face, even if we know that these can be more easily managed (Baran and Woznyj 2020).

In response to the evolution of VUCA, Grabmeier (2020) has further developed the observation to describe the contemporary situation as now being Brittle, Anxious, Non-linear and Incomprehensible (BANI). BANI does offer a more nuanced description of the many challenges we now face as well as providing a target for what we should be seeking to gain individually, collectively and organisational from our actions. If we are in a BANI and VUCA world, then our goals individually and collectively should be to counter the situation and aim towards actions, decisions and perspectives that promote Flexibility, Understanding, Stability and Yearning (FUSY), an acronym that is not just presented as the antonyms of BANI or VUCA but as a set of attributes that in combination can be realised organisationally and individually to counter the negative effects of the external environment on an organisation. It is an acronym that reoccurs throughout this book as a marker of the actions required for a variety of challenges and contradictions. The FUSY counter-response is representative of the fine balance that exists between the negative and positive consequences of any decision in attempting to resolve an issue. For example, the desire to be flexible can lead to incomprehensibility and complexity and a yearning to know more could contribute to anxiety when answers are being sought amongst the ambiguities of artificial intelligence or within an organisation that has a knowledge management system entirely internalised in the minds of its employees.

This initial chapter introduces visual management as one aspect of the FUSY counter-response to the challenges presented by a persistently VUCA/BANI world. Visual management is described as a way of creating an holistic system of knowledge management and exchange that can be applied within an organisation of any size. Visual management encourages a stability of representation that brings genuine understanding and the appropriate yearning to pursue further details and depth when necessary. For clarity, visual management is presented as the management of organisations using visual techniques rather than 'just' the management of visual – artistic – organizations, although it is equally relevant to this sector too.

The overall benefit of visual management is the clarity and connections that can be made between an organisation's operations, strategy and vision. In any organisation, each of these levels must interact with the BANI world, but often the greatest challenge is to ensure that each of these levels align seamlessly and operate with one another (Bergeron et al. 2004). While this type of internal tension has always been identifiable, the noted rise of 'startup culture' (Koskinen 2020) has further reinforced the need for an organisation to function in a wholly integrated manner. Recent examples of business failures that were bursting with vision but had no operations (Cantamessa et al. 2018) are obvious early casualties in terms of longevity. Startups that are not able to develop a strategic direction are generally short-term propositions or invariably end up suffering from the negative influences of the founder effect (Fleising 2002). At the other end of the spectrum, well-established businesses, particularly those that are family-based, may struggle to grow or survive when their focus is on perpetuating their operations without ever defining a clear vision (Allio 2004). While visual management is not a panacea to all these challenges, the awareness and perspectives that it demands give positive impetus to align these different views of the same organisation (Figure 1.1).

Visual management is presented as a tool in the broadest anthropological sense of the term, as a positive extension that is delivered beyond innate human biological capabilities (Wynn 1994). The definition of a tool has been the source of long-term debate, with edge examples and discussions of the place of the art object (Overing 1996) that disrupt the core intent of this definition. For a discussion of visual management, accepting this definition from Wynn can helpfully incorporate language as a culturally shaped and shared tool that enables communication between humans (Parkin 1996).

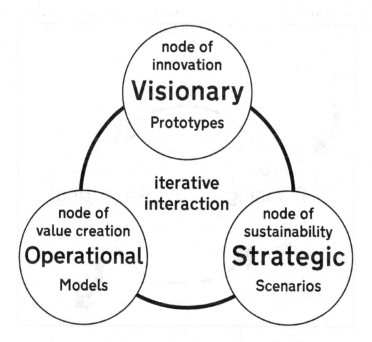

Figure 1.1 The challenge of internal organisational alignment (after Bell et al. 2013)

This statement implies a further challenge of defining what is meant by culture. Culture is highly problematic as a term (Williams 2015) and throughout the book, the term is admittedly used somewhat interchangeably with organisational culture. However, the intended meaning is a shared set of practices, understandings, knowledge, language and identity among a group of people. In an organisational context, this might focus on informal and formal communications and processes, but the intention is that it is read as a more pervasive and prevailing form of shared connections.

Recognising language as a cultural tool is necessary, as visual management uses an organisational language that integrates a continuous feedback loop between vision, planning and reporting, as well as between the qualitative and quantitative elements of an organisation. Developing and evolving a coherent visual language for the organisation reinforces internally learned patterns of success by holding a mirror to its own culture and by being an expression of itself (Figure 1.2).

This last statement requires unpacking through existing exhibits of practice. Partial examples can be drawn from the vanguard of tools that are already available for visual management. These tools include Osterwalder and Pigneur's (2013) Business Model Canvas and subsequent developments, such as the Value Proposition Canvas (Osterwalder et al. 2014). The use of visual management techniques and its potential is exemplified through Lima's *Visual Complexity* (2011) and McCandless's *Information is*

Figure 1.2 The role of visual management within an organisation

Beautiful (2012), *Knowledge is Beautiful* (2014) and *Beautiful News* (2021) as well as the subreddit social media channel dataisbeautiful (reddit.com/r/dataisbeautiful/) that is clearly inspired by this body of work. Entire sectors of activity, including architecture, reveal the value and importance of visual approaches to conducting business. The combination of architectural drawings and plans draws together the qualitative and quantitative aspects of the discipline through visual means. Improved technology and the use of digital twins (Miehe et al. 2021) now enable advanced modelling and virtual walkthroughs of a completed, furnished, even lived building before any physical element is in place. The digital twin permits zooming in to any specific parameter to check its mechanical suitability for the job (Miehe et al. 2021). It is almost impossible to imagine an architectural project being successfully commissioned through a presentation involving a solely text-based description of the intended outcome, accompanied by a lengthy list of the dimensions and the mechanical properties of the proposed materials.

Developing the definition further from this small set of examples, the common language of visual management promotes a people-centric view of the organisation that is understandable to all its employees simultaneously. Earlier theorisations regarding the role and value of visualisation emphasise this benefit. The work of Tufte (2006, 2006a) in identifying the attributes of high-quality visualisations and the Isotype language developed by the Neurath (1937) and others (Neurath and Kinross 2009) evidence the wider capacity and preference for people to communicate and learn in visually stimulating ways. Otto Neurath's heritage as a philosopher of language (Rutte 1991) is one indication of the depth of consideration that was applied to the way that meaning is conveyed through visual languages, including Isotype. Significantly, Marie Neurath contributed the identification of the 'transformer' as a pivotal human role within the process of developing and translating data into meaningful graphical representations. Many of the principles of Isotype can still be found in visual representations that are used (Figure 1.3), and many of these principles link to the exemplars identified by Tufte (2006).

The argument for the value of visual approaches is recognisable in popular culture too. As with so many aspects of how organisations work and interact with their own people, the use of visually oriented communications lags far behind more popular (non-work) usage. Television consumption has been a primary source of entertainment for individuals in advanced economies for over 60 years. The development of YouTube into the second most visited website globally, coupled with the rapid expansion of other streaming services, has evolved the traditional service of broadcast television, but it remains a model that is primarily visual (and audio) in its format.

In contrast, there is pre-COVID evidence to show people aged 15–44 on average spend less than 10 minutes per day outside of work or education

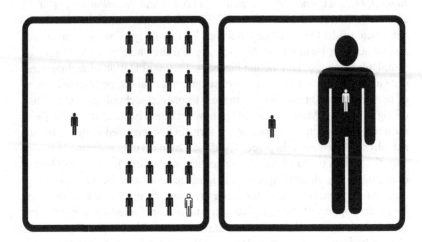

Figure 1.3 Comparing an ISOTYPE principle (left) with an alternative possible
representation. The coarse scaling in the second does not clearly convey
that one person in 24 is being identified

engaged in reading (comfyliving.net/reading-statistics/). It is not a coinci-
dence that this is the same age group in which YouTube viewing is the
most popular. However, COVID did change this situation with recent sta-
tistics suggesting an increase in reading activity reversing a 15-year decline
(National Literacy Trust 2020) with 55.9% of children in the UK reading
weekly and enjoying it (27.6%). Despite a pandemic uplift, this still relatively low level of reading engagement for entertainment begs the question
as to what extent the time spent during the working day reading corporate
reports, strategy documents and operational plans is effective. More concerning is the statistic that 21% of adults in the US and 16.4% of UK adults
(literacytrust.org.uk/parents-and-families/adult-literacy/) have low literacy
levels. It might be assumed that few of these adults will be present in a
boardroom, but when strategy is translated into direct actions – as a text-
based document – there is little chance that any identifiable success that is
reported up an organisation's hierarchy will align with strategic objectives.
Challenges of this type are created *within* the organisation because of the
complexity of the textual documents that are *produced* by the organisation.
A key benefit of visual management is its relationship to strategy development and its implementation. The benefit is premised on the basis that any
organisation's strategy first sets out – in a multitude of ways – to reduce
any forms of VUCA/BANI that can be found within the organisation (Fenton et al 2020). Focus on creating a FUSY organisation requires a clarity

of strategic purpose to be communicated to everyone within the organisation and potentially in many ways that can accommodate multiple learning styles. As a second step, strategy then sets out the ways in which an organisation will gain advantage within the external VUCA/BANI environment against already identified competitors (and acknowledging that some competitors cannot be identified in a VUCA environment). Setting out the advantage requires the value proposition offered by the organisation to be clearly communicated externally to the stakeholders, who will be the specific beneficiaries of this value proposition (Osterwalder et al. 2014).

Acknowledging the continuous presence of VUCA in any organisational context encourages maintaining strategic focus. While the development and application of a strategy is a commonplace affair for organisations of all types, the underlying primary purpose of strategy is traditionally regarded as the need to plan with sufficient foresight to encourage change and to bring about a positive impact on the organisation itself (Davies 2000). There is a nuanced difference between these two positions. The shift in focus is towards addressing the threat of internal VUCA while acknowledging the presence of an external VUCA environment over which very little influence can be directed. This is a new perspective on the same challenge. In this way, strategy is as much a plan for the future as it is a buffer and a mechanism by which to address ever-present, unknown and unavoidable challenges. Being able to move as an organisation from a known current state to a planned future state that exists within the VUCA world has an impact in terms of how developing a strategy might progress. The difference can be more clearly expressed by adopting a visual approach to management. Reducing VUCA within the business involves recognising the internal audience and communicating in a clear way – including a preference for brevity, as there are definite limits to the extent that most employees yearn to know the details of a strategy beyond the key headlines. The history and evolution of advertising (Turner 1965) already shows that articulating a value proposition to an intended audience is best undertaken with visual devices. Bringing the approach and attention previously reserved for generating marketing collateral inside the organisation is not a major shift in thinking for many larger businesses, but it may represent an entirely new further challenge for those that are smaller, rely on word-of-mouth or simple continuity of existence at the heart of their promotion activities.

The argument regarding the meaning and role of visual management that is explored through this book embeds the argument that there is a need to better integrate the relationship of strategy and vision with the management and everyday activities conducted within an organisation. This is the contradiction between creating a stable organisation and one that is flexible enough to respond to the unexpected. There is an implied advocacy in this statement for greater transparency and openness within management practice. Advocacy of this type extends to an emphasis on the benefits of better overall communications within an organisation to encourage its continuous transformation as well as generating understanding and a general yearning from its people to explore new possibilities. To achieve these wider aims, this book takes the view that using visualisations – whether it is in the form of emojis, diagrams or just better use of tabular text – consistently is a necessary key step in achieving change that creates a more resilient and robust organisation that can succeed in a heavily digitalised VUCA environment.

The view of visualisation that is taken throughout is a positive one, and its role within the wider organisation is seen in the same way. Visualisation is regarded as an integral and intimate part of the organisation that remains often undervalued and regarded as being secondary to the development and key workings of an organisation. In contrast, the underlying argument being presented is that visualisations, when presented consistently, accurately and simply, are key artefacts for an organisation and, as such, are central to its success (or otherwise) (Szafir 2018). An artefact-based view of visualisation is itself not new, particularly in software engineering or project management (Lima et al. 2016), nor is the position that visualisation is central to an organisation's success or understanding of itself (Berinato 2016). However, building upon this existing knowledge, what is presented here attempts to integrate multiple threads of thinking drawn from different disciplines that all relate to visualisation and its place within the organisation. Drawing together these threads reflects my own personal experience from over 30 years and is a result of an almost museulogical approach to collating the development of digital technologies and their outputs. Out of these observations comes the perspective that an Excel spreadsheet or a Word document are artefacts themselves that reflect the organisation and the organisational culture that produced them. The role of organisational culture in producing this form of material culture is a perspective not often explored through traditional business and management research (Rathje 1979) with some notable exceptions in relation to retail consumption (Bath 1981). And yet, the material culture of an organisation – including its strategies – is not far removed from describing the artefacts associated with a specific traditional culture, which was a key activity of anthropologists through much of the 20th century and into the current one. Many insights into an organisation can be extracted when the anthropologist's gaze is directed onto a single isolated artefact. What this gaze could interpret from an examination of a single strategy document is an insightful thought experiment. A strategy document might be interpreted under this type of scrutiny as a highly ritualised document intended for possession by a privileged elite but rarely edited or read after its initial production and formal approval. The same interpretation may continue to speculate on the relationship of the strategy document to the known conditions of the world at the time of its production and reason that it reveals a tighter connection with the organisation's own past rather than its relationship and place in the contemporary world that was around it.

The pressures of the current VUCA world have reinforced the power and importance of visualisation to help manage organisations and individuals. Our 'regularly' consumed visualisations continue to be delivered during even the most adverse periods. The nightly synoptic chart during the weather report and the current prices and movements on the world's stock markets are regular components of television news bulletins. Both charts offer safe and familiar pictures of daily activity even if their representations do not necessarily convey accurately a situation at any given moment. Neurath's motto, 'It is better to remember simplified images than to forget exact figures' (Forrest 2020) applies to both representations. While a casual audience will observe an upward or downward dip in the stock chart or an icon for sun, rain or snow, there are many dimensions of meaning packed into these regularly observed formats. Both offer connection, familiarity and a sense of certainty despite the most extreme weather or market conditions. But newer visualisations now demand our attention with even greater urgency. Charts of COVID-19 infection rates and the R-rate have drifted from the public imagination to be almost immediately replaced by maps of Ukraine, its major cities and highways and ominous red arrows indicating the progress of Russian forces. Some of the most insightful representations have been generated during this most recent period of upheaval as well as some of the worst, most meaningless examples of what Tufte labels 'chartjunk' (Tufte 1983). The influence of visualisations despite their status as chartjunk was epitomised during Donald Trump's presidency with the use of simple decision tree charts to justify the success of his testing response in the early stages of the pandemic and other visualisations on which he based his claims that the US response was 'world leading' – irrespective of what that term means or the criteria upon which it might be based. With increasingly digitalised data collection processes, many of these (good and bad) examples develop from raw data into a final visual representation without passing through an intermediary text-based phase. The reality of a direct process, from accessing data to its visual representation, reinforces the importance of the role and skills of the people who can act as the transformers in this process. While much can be automated in these transitions from obtaining data to the presentations of insights, there is still a need for decisions that determine the emphasis and alignment with the overall message that is being conveyed. By taking the material culture view, further insight can be recognised. With each chart being an artefact of a broadcaster or a politician, it can be seen that each item tacitly echoes the strategy, operations and culture of that organisation. This consciously anthropological thread is not the only one being presented. There is a conscious development of the awareness associated with the graphic designer's 'eye'. Several of the authors already cited have dual roles that reveal their hybrid – transformer – skills. Edward Tufte is presented as both statistician and artist. Marie Neurath is described by biographers as a graphic designer. David McCandless is a journalist and information designer. These individual examples of advocates for visual representation are often associated with the possession of artistic skills. The skills and purpose of the designer 'eye' are, in many ways, undervalued within traditional business and management research. The results of a graphic designer's actions are generally relegated to being an outcome of an organisational need, most probably within its marketing plan, rather than as an integral skill connected to organisational success. There are exceptions, but these exceptions do not automatically include all businesses in the arts sector. Somewhat closer scrutiny is required of the extent to which any business *functions* visually rather than just producing visual outputs for clients or satisfying a business need. Consideration of the extent to which an 'eye' exists within the organisation is seen in its application to annual reports, internal communications or a corporate dashboard as more important indicators than whether the company's core purpose is to create comic books, YouTube animations or greeting cards.

Many authors, including those already referenced, have developed arguments promoting the value of information graphics and their role in shaping an organisation and its practise. Tufte succinctly describes it as the experience of 'escaping flatland' (Tufte 1990). The value of 'beautiful' representations of data reveals growing maturity regarding the importance of the designer's 'eye', but few authors who adopt this perspective develop the argument any further to argue for a prioritisation of visual communications across organisations with solely textual documents becoming the technology of last resort. Of course, the argument being made is not a case of completely removing words from the boardroom. Marie Neurath (Neurath and Kinross 2009) describes Isotype, 'as a helping language: some words of explanation are necessary in any chart. To create a language of signs . . . was something we never tried to do.' This is wisdom that can be applied with any advocacy for visual management. The waxing and waning centrality of the design role within organisational practice echoes the various fraught efforts to create 'universal' graphical languages that can convey meaning efficiently and effectively, not just across an entire organisation but across cultures. The failure of these languages to gain traction in the ways they were intended is not a negative judgement on the designers involved, but rather a lesson in what aspects of communications tools and technologies can or cannot be 'designed'. The unrealised aspiration of Blissymbols to create a completely graphical language draws upon the same form of thinking that created Esperanto. Offering a set of visual characters that people find value in using in their own way is commonplace, whereas designing the entire set of rules, structures and characters of a language is a more restrictive offer when existing tools and technologies already exist and are in regular use. As a result, despite the difficulties of learning English, English is the *de facto* language of global trade rather than Esperanto. While some of these earlier attempts at creating visual systems of communication have now become relatively unknown and obscure, the success of emojis within electronic communication, even though sometimes described as quirky or generationally specific, are already a more lasting monument to creating the opportunities – rather than the rules – for a visual language. Over a nearly 30-year history, emojis have generated much discussion as well as some research around their potential benefits and value as a form of written language (Alshenqeeti 2016). Arguably a key factor in this success is precisely because the character set does not come already burdened with any expected rules or syntax. Emojis act more as a type of desire path in communication (Nichols 2020) with a user balancing ease of use with the hope that the meaning is sufficiently conveyed to the intended audience. It is possible to take this very loose association with the formalities of any language even further for emojis. Most emojis are direct representations of a physical object or expression, but the human capacity to layer multiple – positive and negative – meanings onto any given symbol is well established for this extensive character set. The capability for analogy is particularly strong with the fruit and vegetable part of the set – because humans are human.

Combining with material culture studies and graphic design are the contributions of architecture and software engineering to the founding discussions of this book. Drawing on a range of diverse disciplines is an appropriate tactic for a discussion positioned within the discipline of management. Management studies is both a 'magpie' discipline in the ways that it continuously draws upon other areas of knowledge to reinvent itself and, at the same time, a reference discipline with clear heritage back to the earliest thinking and works linked to economics. The many advances in management studies over the last 100 years can be attributed to this existence across a long continuum of knowledge as a home for broad critique, as well as the place for translation and integration between multiple disciplines. More recently, management studies has become a disruptor with increasing integration of more digitally oriented, technical disciplines. The blurring of the social sciences, humanities and science, as well as the quantitative and qualitative, even contributes to the questioning of any neat delineations of individual disciplines as appropriate representations of human knowledge (Pryor and Crossouard 2010). Digital transformation does not just bring benefits to business, but may well force further reconsideration of how we categorise the individuals 'bins' of knowledge.

The role of software engineering is pivotal to the increasing digitalisation of business and management. However, it is through this discipline's direct contributions of a pattern language (Gamma et al. 1994) and the visually oriented Unified Modelling Language (UML) that its key contributions can be identified to this discussion. Similarly, the original discussion of a pattern language for architecture by Alexander et al. (1977) is instructive for the purpose of delivering consistent practice from a seemingly infinite range of opportunities and options that exist within a domain of knowledge in order to undertake a specific action or task. The value of possessing a robust pattern language is drawn upon heavily later in this book (Chapter 5) to bring together the threads introduced in this chapter and to argue for a coherent approach to knowledge that can be confidently positioned as a core aspect of visual management.

The final thread of thought found in this work is closely affiliated with the information systems worldview. The advocacy for an integrated approach based on the idea of a system is the pivotal underlying theorisation expressed throughout this work. A single theorisation that is powerful and illuminating and shows a bias in the arguments presented here in being from my own 'home' discipline. But, given the observation foregoing about the value of disciplines (Pryor and Crossouard 2010), that may be highly significant or irrelevant as a discussion point. What is often undervalued within the information systems perspective is the due attention that is given to software, hardware and data as well as the aspects of people, communications and processes. In other words, the classic model of an information system continues to have value as a coherent system of thought for building understanding of the organisation and its response to the VUCA/BANI world. The work of information systems researchers provides a significant body of theorisation regarding the role of each of the six components found in any system that relates directly to the overall success, impact and sustainability of any organisation. The view that any organisation is itself a complete system (or information system) offers direction for understanding how the relationship of the components plays out in relation to a visual management perspective.

It is primarily through an information systems perspective that the importance of visualisation in the organisations is drawn out. The system perspective supports a justification of the need to maintain an holistic and integrated view of the organisation. Visualisation and visual representations are clearly an aspect of the communications element of the system. At the same time, visualisations are an output from the software and data of the organisation. Visual representations inform business processes and ultimately help people to undertake the demands of their own professional role. These observations of the many ways in which visualisation and visual representations play within an organisation are at the core of this book. Picking out the people in the system is reiterated continuously. The beneficial role of visualisation and visual techniques for people will persist irrespective of the technical advancement of artificial intelligence or machine learning. There will continue to be a case and a need for decision-making to be made by people, no matter how automated or data-driven an organisation becomes. The human ability to make decisions that are contrary to the available evidence is key to humans' relevance and role in management situations dominated by artificial intelligence. In fact, in a purely automated organisation – for example, a distributed autonomous organisation (DAO) (Nissen et al. 2017) or another yet-to-be-imagined new organisational form – it may well be that the contrary decisions made by humans will create the key distinction between one organisation and the next within the same sector. To this extent, a perverse decision made by a human may produce an outcome that defines a new business model or breaks the prevailing algorithms of orthodoxy. The current reality is that a human making decisions based on his or her own instincts, even when it is aligned with the data available, will result in a different path from an organisation where a different human is making different decisions. Returning to the material culture perspective, focusing on the people within the organisation – the system – positions visualisation as pivotal in helping to inform decisions because these visualisations are coherent, meaning-laden artefacts produced, created and curated by the organisation itself. Such a view could be dismissed as a self-serving agenda with the result that these actions build an organisational echo chamber. However, taking a coherent approach strengthens the idea that an organisation's primary strategic purpose is to protect itself from the external VUCA environment. Gathered data that can be transformed into accurate insights regarding the external world through visualisations are important tools in achieving this strategic goal. This position implies a progressive view of the organisation by shaping a place where its people – owners, managers or employees – are all supported and protected. Taking this view balances supporting the organisation's people as the first strategic priority of an organisation with the second, which is the need to collaborate and interact with the external world.

In developing this argument for the importance of a positive organisational culture with shared communications tools, this book explores the surprisingly long history of visualisation in relation to management tools and techniques that ultimately comes to an important juncture with current corporate dashboards. The dashboard is equally celebrated and lamented here. By bringing data to the point of visualisation for an organisation, they are an example of the richness that could be possible with visual management, but many are now in a state where they represent an opportunity lost in terms of their design, delivery and utilisation. Taking an artefact-oriented perspective does offer some explanations as to why corporate dashboards are in this situation with their lack of integration into the overall organisational culture and a resulting sense that the visualisations are not really 'owned' by the organisation. In fact, with the most extreme cases, corporate dashboards may show a representation of the organisation that is unfamiliar to the organisation itself and that exists, in many ways, despite that organisation.

Brought together, all these threads hint at the direction and conclusions that this book pursues. While it may not be a grand claim, an organisation's ability to visually manage and be visually managed will only come about when the tools for creating these communications are an ingrained and integral aspect of that organisation's day-to-day operations. The result is that the prospect of enabling visual management with an organisation will be possible when tools such as Microsoft Word and Microsoft Excel can take a stream of data (or a line of thinking) and present it in ways that can be understood by the entire organisation while reflecting the culture of that organisation. The technological barriers to the implementation of visual management are not far from being overcome and may arguably already have occurred.

Despite such an extensive preamble, this book sets out a straightforward thesis. It argues that with the increasing maturity of digital tools that are capable of visualisation combined with increased awareness that existing and traditional techniques of management may not be sufficiently capable of delivering the desired results, there is an opportunity to work with primarily visual artefacts as an effective way of managing and leading the organisation. It is a thesis premised on a range of assumptions. The core assumption is that it is only now that digital technologies and particularly visualisation technologies have come within the reach of any sized organisation in a way that they can be used effectively without specialist training or knowledge. The second premise is that it is a human tendency to prefer to learn with visual imagery rather than solely text-based description. The implication is that a fully mature visual management technique would be able to convey all the insight needed through various combinations of visual artefacts without needing to resort to lengthy multi-page documents of solely text that ultimately may never end up being read or fully understood by the intended audience. The final premise is the most theoretical. It is argued that all the outputs of software and of management create a set of artefacts that are particular and unique – in combination – to that organisation. An artefact-based perspective of the organisation and its management is a somewhat challenging one in that it places these outputs central to the actual shape, definition and meaning of the organisation rather than being outcomes or inconsequential and disposable aspects of day-to-day operations. Taking a material cultural perspective and applying it to the organisation extends existing thinking around organisational culture by recognising and emphasising the role of artefacts within an organisation as being important, meaning-laden and action-shaping. These artefacts provide longevity to thoughts and ideas and enable the presence of individuals who have long left the organisation to still be felt through these tangible proxies. The material culture aspects of an organisation are generally undervalued within organisational culture discussions to such an extent that 'unknown' influences within organisational culture are sometimes puzzled upon by scholars (Owens and Steinhoff 1989) because they fail to recognise or acknowledge the presence of 'things' all around them.

2 A short history of the long evolution towards visual management

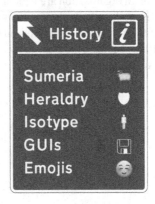

Visual management is not new practice even if the specific term has not entered regular usage. This chapter sketches a timeline of visual management over an historically long epoch. The story consciously jumps between the proto-Sumerian methods for tracking herds and ideographic languages through heraldry and pipe rolls and incorporates the development of cartography as a political tool. This intersects with the examination of more recent developments that support visual management that can be discovered in the development of the standard graphical user interface (GUI) on personal computers and mobile devices. The most recent development of emojis as a standard visual toolkit for communications on all computing devices is further indication of the direction that visual management will evolve in the future. The last stage of this long evolution is linked to the observations in the previous chapter regarding the increasing maturity of Microsoft Excel as the bellwether tool for popularising visual techniques as a viable tool for the management of organisations.

Within the selective history identified in this chapter is the reiteration of the human capacity to visually communicate meaningfully in many different

DOI: 10.4324/9781003304166-2

forms and contexts. Text is an intimate part of this representation but in a way where words, numbers and sometimes sentences are framed as part of an overall visual device rather than within the structures of paragraphs, sections or chapters. One instructive example of this use of text in conjunction with a visually oriented document is the historical atlas. Gilbert's (2011) *The Routledge Atlas of British History* offers nearly 200 maps that chart 2,000 years of British history. The maps alternate between zooming in to particular areas within the British Isles and zooming out to a continental or global view. Text is employed to label locations, frame specific important events and provide a key for the solely monochromatic maps. Such a collection provides an accessible means to digest a vast swath of British history that would support most learners for at least half of the UK's current GCSE History qualification (AQA 2022). Visual representations channel the human capacity to learn and understand in ways that are consistent, sustainable and generally more successful (McKendrick and Bowden 1999; Smith and Blankinship 2000).

Taking these claims into the realm of management practice is a means to introduce visual management and to emphasise the importance of the material culture of an organisation in shaping its collective actions, thinking and overall presentation of itself. And what is offered here is by no means a comprehensive history of visualisation. It is not intended to be presented in that way. By exploring a range of visual techniques that have been used within social and economic contexts, it is possible to show how regularly this approach is used and is evidence of the much wider scale that a more complete and comprehensive recounting would entail. As a result of these limitations, what is presented is a piecemeal and non-linear collection of indicative examples where visualisation has played an important role in the actions of organisations and in shaping nations. Many of these examples evidence the ways that visual approaches have come to define the way that social, culture and geographic entities are understood within popular and mainstream thinking.

The vignettes presented here do not necessarily represent the entire historical context in which these examples are positioned. However, their descriptions may prompt the reader to explore the specific topic in more detail. While this exploration will be rewarding for the subject material itself, it serves to reinforce rather than diminish the point of the argument being presented here regarding the importance of the visual in management. The intention is to prompt further thinking around the key premise of this book. In other words, the artefacts of visual management are an ever-present and powerful aspect of human societies which even predate what is now defined as written literacy. As the narrative of early languages reveals, written literacy itself slowly evolved out of earlier systems with the textual representations of each letter being abstractions or abbreviations for earlier and more directly visual representations. Looking at a formal document produced in the 21st century for a large multinational corporation or a national government and seeing within the many repeated characters that are being used a squiggle of water, an ox head, a waving hand or the body of a fish is certainly a challenging realisation of the longer social history that every letter embeds without necessarily diminishing the potential gravity with which that document should be read (Figure 2.1).

Visual management describes a technique of managing an organisation that utilises primarily visual artefacts in ways that are integral to its core purpose and mission. The claims and benefits of visual management are made irregularly by scholars (Roberts and Laramee 2018) but its practise happens on a daily basis in all parts of the world in different ways and effectively without the need for theorisation or reflection. Critiques exist for some aspects of the underlying notions for creating a visual language. DeFrancis (1984) argues that the European myth of the ideographic nature of Chinese Pinyin writing was a key motivation that led to misguided efforts to develop new ideographic languages in Europe right into the 20th century. Criticism is particularly directed at the Blissymbols semasiographic – or writing with signs (Unger and DeFrancis 1995) – language proposed by Charles Bliss (Sproat 2016). The ambition as well as the brittleness of the concept is well expressed in an essay 'One Writing for One World' (Dreyfuss 1984) that offers a sampler of some of the symbols proposed (Table 2.1) and helpfully suggested that all the symbols could be represented on an IBM ball typewriter or through typesetting (both now long disused technologies). From the 100 basic symbols Bliss outlines in *Semantography* (1978) there are a further 882 pages of symbol combinations that represent concepts in communications, science and business. Adopting a prescriptive approach is the hallmark of a constructed language and, at the same time, is a definite indication of why the system is not now in common usage.

However, the subsequent development and popularisation of digital technology diminishes some of the relevance of previous critiques for the creation of a universal constructed visual language. The availability of digital

Figure 2.1 Proto-Sinaitic characters used to render the modern English word 'meet'. The derivation of the word itself is different, but the connection of two people with raised hands appears particularly apt

(Source: usefulcharts.com/products/evolution-of-the-alphabet)

Table 2.1 A sampler of Blissymbols, their meanings and location within currently available symbol fonts

Symbol	□	૭	♥
Represents	Paper	Ear	Heart
Meaning	Page	Hearing	Emotion
Location	Wingdings 2 at character 0 (zero)	Webdings at Character O (the Blissymbol is more stylised as a single curve)	Webdings at character Y (the Blissymbol is more symmetrical and hollow)

Table 2.2 Different types of written forms

	Ideogram/graph	*Pictogram/ graph*	*Logogram/graph*	*Phonogram/ graph*
Definition	A symbol that represents an idea or object	A symbol that looks like the thing it is intended to represent.	A symbol that represents a word – also lexigraph (also syllabogram for syllables)	A symbol that represents a sound in the language
Example	☢	☺	$	A

authoring tools and reading devices now makes ideographic expression simpler to author and to access. The ability to inscribe visually is coupled with a new need for written ideographic language. The information over-load produced by the digitalisation of organisations, business and society creates new motivation to explore ways to manage and address the volume, variety, velocity and veracity of information that is now available to us all individually. The ready availability and widespread use of logographic and pictographic symbols on a computing device means that there is greater flexibility, understanding and stability around the use of these visual sym-bols in combination with text than in any early period when, for example, complete systems such as Blissymbols were introduced. It is even possible to suggest that there is now a yearning to use what could now be regarded as a simpler form of written expression – through the flexible use of emojis as well as ideograms, logograms and other pictograms (Table 2.2).

Although the book is classified as 'Humour', Civaschi and Milesi's (2013) *Life in five seconds* offers examples of one-page stories that sum-marise the histories of famous people, events and monuments. Using exist-ing pictographic typefaces and common logograms, each story provides a witty overview of the key moments in each narrative. The relative ease with which these stories can be interpreted suggests that more symbols have entered common use with broadly agreed-upon shared meaning since Bliss's project. The general use of tools such as graphical user interfaces on computing devices may have already instructed us to be more flexible in our interpretation of symbols in order to be able to 'fill in the gaps'.

Jumping backwards, with the use of proto-Sumerian 6,000 years ago we see the first documented pictographic language by which the accounting of livestock could be done accurately and in a way that was considered fair by both buyer and seller (Friberg 1984). The starting point was using clay tokens to physically represent the trade items being exchanged. With each token representing a trade item, the next step in its development was to bake these tokens into a clay pillow, creating a form of contract. Having to break the clay pillow to see the contents became a time-consuming process and apocryphally is the source of the phrase, 'breaking the contract' (Mercer 1913). The act of drawing a picture of the contents of the pillow onto the soft clay before it was baked reveals the beginning of proto-Sumerian cuneiform script. The next leap in innovation was to recognise that the physical tokens inside the baked clay were not needed if their symbols were written onto the pillow itself. Simplifying the system improved the speed of conducting a transaction. Recognising that combinations of existing symbols could be brought together to represent more ideas and that new symbols themselves could be constructed to represent more abstract or complex thoughts brings the story through to the development of Sumerian cuneiform and the formal beginning of one of the earliest written languages. Further stylisation creates abstract letters now fully detached from the original clay tokens that they once represented. Further technological innovations occurred over many centuries and influenced the development of different cultures across the Sumerian region of influence (Gnanadesikan 2009).

To put this in a simpler way, pictures preceded what we now recognise as words. As languages change and become formalised and more consistent, there is an impact on how they shape people's thinking and practices (Robbeets et al. 2021). Many debates exist about the ways that speakers of different languages think in different ways (Boroditsky 2011) and similarly how the formalising of language practice through national education programmes influences the construction of class sentiment (Johnson 1970) and the levelling out of regional language variants. Written, spoken and drawn forms of language are dynamic, as even relatively recent changes in spelling preference for individual words can shew (Lehmann 1992). Although a written language is not synonymous with culture (culture precedes literacy), its definition of shared lifeways through common symbols, meanings and practices means that it does have a significant influence. Rather than becoming enmeshed in the deeper academic debates about the form of written language, the key observation being made here is that meaning can be readily presented and transferred through visual devices just as readily now as it was 6,000 years ago.

This timeline could more speculatively be stretched back further. It may be possible to claim that cave paintings such as those found at Lascaux in France and dating from 17,000 years ago are even earlier examples of a visual guide for the movement and hunting of wild cattle at the time and can be read as a form of early hunting manual for subsequent generations (Leroi-Gourhan 1982). The paintings are artefacts that encapsulate the most pressing concerns of life and death at the time. However, at this span of time since their creation, any meaning that could be interpreted from our own perspective and knowledge will remain largely speculation. Recent research has discovered that many cave images include the hands of children, suggesting that what we now see could be the remains of (instructive) leisure time spent by a family (Cascone 2022).

At the other bookend of this history, the most recent form of pictograph is easily recognised and has already been mentioned. Emojis are evidence of the formation of the newest visual system of representation. The value of emojis is found in the need to communicate with minimal keystrokes irrespective of language (or dialect) around the world in the era of immediate internet-based communication. The motivation for the development is not so much the lack of a common language, as English arguably represents the internet's current *lingua franca* (Vettorel 2014), but the need to represent common nouns and some verbs with the fewest keystrokes on devices that offer no tactile response or have a confined physical form that prohibits the use of a full keyboard. It could even be argued that the lack of formal typing training within formal education – the typewriter classes of the 20th century – has further inspired this development of emojis as an 'easy' new visual form of expression. The evolution of emojis towards becoming a new visual communication has not occurred overnight. It is possible to trace the history of emojis back over 25 years and perhaps not surprising, given the ideographic nature of Kanji, emojis originated in Japan with the SoftBank company (Burge 2019). Determining the origins of the emoji set itself is a somewhat moot point within the overall history of visual representations using keyboards. Emojis clearly have a linkage to the earlier emoticons that were used in Japan, Europe and North America from the early 1980s, during the highpoint of bulletin board system (BBS) usage (Derks et al. 2008). Bulletin board systems were a significant precursor to the wider availability of the internet outside academic and military usage as well as preceding the creation of the World Wide Web. Emoticons still appear in some communications and despite reaching a form of high art at their peak in the 1980s, there is still a clear relationship between the simplest emoticons and the most used emojis. So although one of the few emoticons that is viewed horizontally representing John Lennon – //0-0\\ – has not made it into the emoji set, a version of Santa *<|:-) has become 🎅 as well as the inevitable and ubiquitous smiley which was once :) but is now 😊. The history of the development of each emoji character reflects the increased ability of computing devices to accurately render any given image accurately or at least in highly stylised accuracy with a great deal of detail packed inside a very small form. It is now even possible with advances in technology to possess a keyboard where each key is a tiny screen capable of displaying any symbol and is completely programmable (www.artlebedev.com/optimus/popularis/).

Emojis invariably make an appearance in many of the subsequent chapters of this book. Such a heavy presence should be expected given the popularity of their use as well as the attempts to create full-length books entirely using emojis. As one example, the emoji translation of Moby Dick by Herman Melville sets out a task for the reader to effectively re-interpret a fully graphical representation back into familiar phrases and narrative (www.emojidick.com). At a more modest level, even a casual examination of most Twitter feeds or WhatsApp groups reveals the important role that emojis have assumed in supporting (or entirely being) the messages.

In the 6,000 years since proto-Sumerian, there can be found many other examples of visual languages, pictographic usage and visualisations that have been used to bring about clarity and simplicity in communications and processes. Many of these devices and systems can be described as effective techniques of management that were used to address the immediate pressing issues of the age. These examples of historical visual management show the ways in which visualisation techniques evolve – just as formal written and spoken languages do – to become highly stylised and on occasion will inform the development of subsequent techniques that are then used for different purposes. For example, the modern development of national flags and the associated symbolism used to visually represent the citizens of a country in peace and wartime can be seen as directly inheriting from the development of the visual language of heraldry during the mediaeval period, a fact readily evidenced at any England football match or during the conflict in Ukraine.

Our own Roman or Latin alphabet has a similar evolutionary heritage from proto-Sinaitic (Figure 2.1) about 3,500 years ago to its current form. With only a little imagination and a slightly tilted head, it isn't difficult to see the origins of our current capital 'A' in a bull's head, the presence of a fish within the letter 'D', a person with upraised arms in the letter 'E' or a squiggle representing water in the letter 'M' (Rainey 1975). Finding reasons for this type of transition is perhaps easier to imagine when assuming the role of the Roman stone carver working with marble and their available technologies. Having to represent these ornate and fluid symbols with hammer and chisel and a very inflexible medium will invariably force changes, including an increased use of straight lines. All technologies adapt continuously to the surrounding environment and circumstances, including the constraints of the tools that enable it (Wynn 1994). An even more radical proposal regarding the interconnections of languages and scripts is that proto-Sinaitic was itself an adaptation of already existing Egyptian hieroglyphics into a different environment and conditions (Haring 2015). If this connection was clearly proven, the evolution of written language to the Latin script would represent a long version of the partial history that is represented in summary by the Rosetta Stone.

As a very loose segue, the period of the Rosetta Stone's modern deciphering was a key period in the rapid maturing of visualisation. The development of modern European society during the 19th century was a period marked by the rise of science and the scientific method. Many science disciplines, such as maths and physics, are well-versed in creating their own logograms to present key values and ideograms for pivotal concepts, but equally important, it is through science that quantitative visualisation methods developed. In the late 19th century, logarithmic graphs, choropleth charts, Venn diagrams and other similar representation devices were all created as mechanisms to ensure the clearer representation of complex data (Edwards 2004). Ultimately most of these devices were intended for making management decisions in one form or another. The common link between many of these visualisation techniques comes from the demands of warfare and disruption through the 18th and 19th centuries, including the Napoleonic Wars and the later Crimean War.

Warfare and the management of warfare have a significant role in the development of visualisation over a much longer period. The development of visual languages during the mediaeval period, including the use of heraldry in Europe (Lewis 1996) and other similar devices in locations such as Japan (Turnbull 2012), show the enduring need for management techniques related to warfare and to the battlefield. Highly visible symbols and colours that are both contrasting and not prone to misinterpretation for an alternative symbol are key criteria in the design of heraldic blazons (Lewis 1996). Being able to distinguish one symbol from another on the battlefield is a clear rationale for the origins of heraldry, but in the development of this visual communication, the artistic and familial relationships that these coats of arms can reveal became equally important. As a result, coats of arms over time could develop into incredibly complex designs with linkages to multiple ancestors being represented on the subdivided fields of the blazon (Ivall 1988). The result is the creation of a visual family history in a way that even now complex family tree software cannot improve upon. The use of charges and coats of arms changed in politer times – or at least in times of less conflict directly involving the landed classes in battle – and on into the early modern period. Individual coats of arms become closely protected and coveted as an indication of higher status and reflect long-standing linkages to location, which builds evidence for the ownership of precious resources across the countryside. As power shifted from the force of arms to the ownership of resources, in England the monarch instructed the creation of Pipe Rolls to assess the taxes owed to them by the gentry, who were recorded on the rolls with their coats of arms (Keats-Rohan 2002).

The development of heraldry into the modern period is closely linked to the management and ownership of the land. A side effect of the way heraldry developed in England is that the simplest coats of arms generally represent those that were awarded or assumed first and visually represent the initial families who were looked upon favourably by the monarch of the period. Later coats of arms, because of the need to be distinctive, became increasingly more complex and even required the introduction of new symbols and more artistic forms of dividing lines in order to create visual difference. The development of heraldry's complexity mirrors an increasing population that included an expanded landed upper class.

But heraldry was not enough and additional technology that could directly support claims of land ownership and the resources found on it became an increasingly urgent need. Measurement technologies enabled more accurate mapping of the countryside on a small scale as well as on a national level. Mapping enabled property owners to set out and define their relationship to other property owners and what they owned. Mapping provided a way to communicate this ownership to a non-literate audience and made a clear statement in legal cases to deflect any alternative claims.

The technologies for mapping links closely to military needs and the desire of emerging nations to either acquire or define themselves in relation to the land they held. The early modern period is hallmarked by a rise in colonialism and the acquisition of land by European powers across the globe. Examples of the importance of mapping in this process can still be seen now as tangible reminders of the inaccuracies of the process at the time, but the importance that was placed on that mapping ensures that the early mistakes have had to be made to work. One example of this inaccuracy is the state boundaries on the East Coast of the United States. Perhaps the most well-known division within the United States is the Mason-Dixon line (Davenport 2004). The route of this line itself is a compromise and a result of errors that were initially made in mapping the east coast of North America. One noticeable adjustment is most visible on the state border of Delaware at its northernmost point where it touches Pennsylvania (Figure 2.2). The

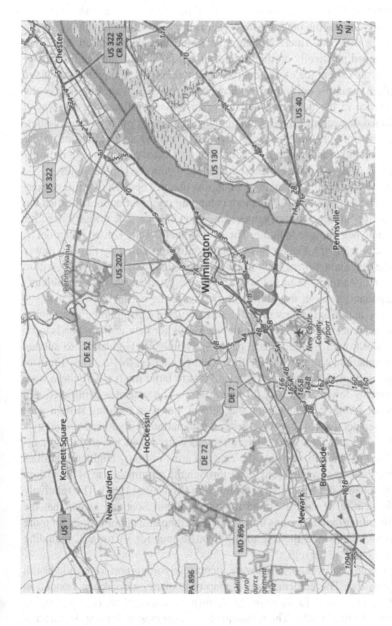

Figure 2.2 The northern border of Delaware

(Source: OpenStreetMaps)

border at this point is part of the circumference of a circle that is centred on the town of New Castle (now absorbed into the Wilmington urban area) and diverts the Mason-Dixon line from its direct East-West alignment. Compromise defines the border. The border is a result of the individual English colonies of North America being granted territory described on paper that overlapped physically on the ground. In less populated parts of the United States, the difference of one degree of latitude in the land grants may have resulted in simple compromises; however, in the Delaware Bay region, the difference in the definition of land grants was significant for the way it included or excluded new populations within one or other of the colonies. The circumference of the circle was itself defined as a resolution to the original land grants and it is this line that now takes precedence in defining one part of the emotive North/South divide within the United States.

In the UK, formal and national mapping practice began as a military exercise. The fact that the UK's national mapping organisation is still called the Ordnance Survey continues to evidence this linkage. The military need for mapping began close to home. The development of the United Kingdom as an entity itself involved a form of colonialism imposed by English power on the other constituent parts of that United Kingdom, most notably within Scotland. At the time of the union, the loyalty shown by many inhabitants of Scotland through the 18th century was to the earlier Stewart dynasty. The resistance to the new monarchy necessitated a programme of mapping that could accurately determine the pathways for new military roads to be pushed through Scotland, and particularly into the Highlands, to subdue its people and to know its configuration (Anderson 2010). The 'English' response to their mapping of Scotland was to build roads where there were previously few or no tracks (Haldane 1962). The project was initiated as a form of military management and control, but road building shifted people's perspectives of their linkages and associations with other communities which had previously been based around water-based travel. In an unexpected link back to heraldry, the coats of arms of many Highland families reinforce their association to water through the prominent use of the birlinn or lymphad – the Viking style sailing ship (Macaulay 1996). The relatively rapid demise of visible armed resistance within Scotland meant that the early military interventions transformed the map into opportunities for more passive actions and the rise of the Scottish tour for Victorians, including Queen Victoria herself.

Mapping and visualisation were increasingly important for public health reasons too. The epidemiological map of cholera outbreaks in London in 1855 eventually led John Snow to identify the source of the outbreak and to prevent further deaths. The technique used a dot map technique. It is a technique that is commonly still seen and used for similar reasons in identifying the individual incidents of community-borne diseases. In Snow's case, it led him to the water pump that was infected by the decaying bodies from a nearby graveyard and enabled him to (illegally) lock the lethal pump – apparently to the outrage of some local citizens at the time (Holzman 2021). Florence Nightingale used visualisation during the Crimean War to document the sanitary conditions being experienced by soldiers. Her technique was to use coxcombs, or rose diagrams, to represent the rate of different causes of death (Brasseur 2005).

The period of the mid-19th century was a rich and productive period for exploring the benefits of visualisation and pushing the limits of creativity. In 1869, Charles Minard created a flow diagram representing Napoleon's march on Moscow (Wainer 2003). Minard's diagram overlaid data on a map stretching from the French borders to Moscow and simultaneously showed the size of the army and its rapid decline as it faced a Russian winter as well as its continued decline during the retreat. Tufte has long championed the use of good visualisation for management and has described this 1869 chart as the best graphic ever produced (Tufte 1983).

As colonial powers themselves transformed from different forms of government towards democracy, the value of mapping expanded. Now, accurate mapping could ensure demographic representation that was equal and fair in relation to the franchised population. Mapping technologies could reassure that the dominant colonial powers could accurately divide up other parts of the world in mutually agreeable ways. Even in a post-colonial world, the impact of this influence is evident across the map of the world. Any suspiciously straight line demarking two countries' borders generally hints at its imposed and colonial origins. These examples of straight lines ignore real topography on the ground and cut through existing and persisting cultural groups (Paine et al. 2021). The southern boundary of Syria where it touches both Jordan and Iraq is one identifiable example (Barr 2011). Few African nations do not have a straight line in their borders for the same reason (First 1970), and even Ethiopia, which escaped the direct attention of colonialism itself, has a boundary with Somalia that reflects international influence on its definition. These examples of visualisation where a boundary was neatly drawn with a ruler in a chancellery in London, Paris or Berlin is clear evidence of how powerful and persistent visualisation can be.

Other new technologies in the late 19th century influenced the visualisations that were being developed and employed. 'Railway mania' introduced a concern for the documentation of the routes and their respective schedules. Charles Ibry's representation of the train route between Paris and Lyon created an innovative visualisation (Rendgen 2019). With his approach, Ibry successfully shows the relative speeds of each train journey on that route and the point at which they arrived at any given station. By visualising the route in terms of its velocity rather than geographically, it is possible to see whether a train will overtake an earlier departure and answers the question asked at some point by all commuters, whether getting on the next train will be the fastest way of getting to their destination. Non-geographical mapping opens a further thread in the history of visualisation with Beck's development of the London Underground map (Garland 1994) and rarer efforts to create more qualitative maps such as Rothuizen's (2014) *The Soft Atlas of Amsterdam* that tackles the mapping of, for example, a student bedroom, pyjama days and a bicycle accident.

The more recent history of visualisation includes the development of graphical user interfaces (GUI) for computing devices. The early 20th century drive to create symbolic and visual systems – including Blissymbols (Bliss 1978) and Isotype (Neurath and Kinross 2009) – still has influence today over popular GUIs. Many symbols that we are familiar with on a day-to-day basis through computing devices were initially defined by these designers. However, there can be risk in using any symbols that are directly linked with technologies in the evolving usage of a (visual) language. Many relatively modern symbols can become ossified by capturing representations of technologies, concepts or ways of thinking that have not kept pace with the evolution of technology itself. In other words, the representation of the tool has itself become archaic because of the way the usage is delivered has continued to evolve. The challenge for visualisation is that the evolution of the technology is often in the direction of becoming less visible or invisible, making a suitable pictogram problematic. Key exemplars of this situation are the continued use of the 3.5-inch floppy disc icon as the generally accepted symbol for saving a file and a physical clipboard for cutting and pasting. Similarly, on mobile 'smart' phones – the symbol used to indicate the phone function is a traditional (corded) landline handset, which is an increasingly rare item. All these earlier technologies fell out of common usage over 20 years ago and for anyone under the age of 25, these symbols that they use on a day-to-day basis must appear anachronistic if indeed their origins or purpose are ever questioned at all. It could even be suggested that these familiar icons have shifted within a generation from being pictograms to ideograms.

Other symbols that we regularly see in a graphical user interface may be regarded with increasing puzzlement when looked at in this artefact-based way. The prevalence of pen icons in many of the Microsoft Office menus seems incongruous for many users when the inscription process is delivered through a physical or software-based keyboard. The Segoe UI font goes even further by offering a symbol for the now rarely used fountain pen nib – ✐.

The desire to create generic visual languages persists. Among the most extensive of these efforts is the Noun Project (thenounproject.com), a massive online collection of icons delivered up by designers from around the world with the express intention of representing nouns as pictograms or ideograms. As an aside, the Noun Project's 2021 April Fool's joke was announced on Medium and promoted the release of their sister site, the Verb Project (medium.com/noun-project/introducing-the-verb-project-d7db814fca8b). While this was a joke, the idea that verbs could be visually represented is itself an equally challenging and compelling thought. A search of the current version of the Noun Project for common verbs such as 'been', 'say' and 'done' does produce results even if some of these are of arguably low relevance. Being able to combine nouns and verbs in a combination of symbols and words is the basis for creating semantics and not just a syntactic understanding. In other words, nouns combined with verbs are the basis for sharing meaning.

One provocative challenge to the attempts at classifying the different scripts of human language as well as being a visual language that has been hiding in plain sight are the many programming languages – a set of visual languages in reverse. As constructed languages, programming languages force a strictness of usage far more rigorous than that imagined by Blis-symbols. Due to the text-based limitations of computing devices in the early development of high-level languages (C, C++, Pascal, Perl, PHP, Python), the symbols that are used usually appear analogous to words. The variables used within a piece of code are arbitrary, but for readability, new users are usually instructed to make them 'meaningful'. Similarly, the fixed structures of a programming language, its logic and control structure tend to utilise symbolic words that explain the purpose, such as 'print' or 'exit'. However, these descriptions are just convenient labels for the underlying instructions that the computer executes. We are using convenient words to represent the meaning of the code to the humans who create it, rather than the computer that compiles and uses it. A hint at the ways in which programming could take a more visual approach to its symbols is the Pythonji extension to the popular Python language. Including the extension in a developer's toolkit enables code to be written in a way in which variable names can be emojis. The result is often more compact code, and with the suitable choice of emoji, the meaning of the code can become clearer (Figure 2.3). Pythonji

```
import pandas as 🐼
🐍 = 🐼.DataFrame(
    {
        "😀": ["🐼", "🐍", "🐛"],
    },
).set_index("😀")
print(🐍)
```

Figure 2.3 Example code using pythonji and emojis

is a practical example of how 'visual' approaches can seamlessly combine using words as well as symbols.

But it is with Microsoft Excel that perhaps the most interest lies in relation to the long development and evolution of visual management approaches. The maturing of Microsoft Excel as a business tool parallels the longer evolution of visual languages. As Microsoft Excel has become more adept at visually representing numbers (and textual data) in useful and clear ways, so too has the ability for organisations to manage themselves through this visually oriented interface. Despite being available for many years, the visual capability of Microsoft Excel is still in its relative infancy and its usage is not fully explored by many organisations.

The history of Excel is the dual development of a tool that provides basic visual management capabilities and the ability for an organisation to be visually managed in a relatively simple way – the relatively mundane action of sharing files between workers. Excel brings together the ability to simultaneously show qualitative and quantitative data. Although primarily a quantitative tool, it is straightforward to 'break' this intention by adding textual descriptions or emojis into cells. Other software is available that can readily combine the qualitative and quantitative, but it is Microsoft Excel that is by far the most popular, most common and most understood of this type of software. Being able to bring together a mixed economy of quantitative data and qualitative representations through a combination of visualisations, whether a logogram, ideogram or pictogram, makes Excel the key tool that sets the criteria for maturing visual management techniques. While it is a claim that would be met with disdain from many competing start-ups and other established software vendors, Microsoft Excel could be regarded in this way as the hallmark technology for visual management. If it is capable of being represented in Microsoft Excel, then the organisation is capable of being visually managed.

The discussion of languages raises a more general concern about the use of visualisations and their use within a management context. It is a question of the clarity of the communication and specifically how fully the meaning of the author is transferred to the reader. An example used by Dreyfuss (1984) suitably highlights this challenge. The image presented is a cartoon-style strip representing three steps. The elements were intended to indicate to miners in South Africa, who at the time were often illiterate, that they should remove any rock or debris found on the train lines. The cartoon first shows a rock on a rail line. Then a worker with a wheelbarrow is shown next to the rock. Finally, the rock is now in the worker's wheelbarrow being removed. However, this cartoon only works if you read from left to right and illiterate miners have no such cultural limitations in their interpretation of the cartoon. As a result, the mine authority discovered an increasing number of rocks appearing on the rail lines as the miners duly performed the task that the cartoon asked of them – when you read the cartoon from right to left. Arguably this example shows the power of visualisation and visual language and in this case its purpose was let down through the imposition of assumptions that came from a literate designer who used a particular style of reading. The solution of adding arrows to point from left to right could have potentially overcome their assumptions so easily.

More recent examples of the culturally specific meanings of visual symbols can be found with emojis. The emoji that is intended to represent the okay symbol – 🤌 – a hand with thumb and forefinger pinched together may clearly indicate this message for some, but in some Asian cultures this means 'pay me', and increasingly in the US this is a symbol used by far-right political groups as a symbol of identification. Given their direct reference to a human body part, it is not surprising that many of the hand gestures in the emoji set have different meanings in different cultures. Likewise, the solidarity emoji – 👌- in Mexico has a much more offensive meaning. The potential for offence cuts in all directions when it comes to cultural differences. So, while Western cultures see the poo emoji – 💩 – with derision and amusement, it is included because of its reference to good luck in Japanese culture (Mei and Boyle 2010).

The appropriation of symbols is a recurrent theme in digital technology. Computer users only need to scan their keyboard to realise that we all regularly use a much wider set of symbols than the 26 letters, 10 digits and 'regular' punctuation. Mac users have a particularly rich set of extra keys, including the command key (⌘) which is arguably based on the symbol for a Swedish campground or a more traditional Scandinavian knot symbol (Noe 2020). Other keyboard options include the paragraph symbol (§) and the option (⌥) symbol that may speculatively represent a railroad switching track (Brownlee 2012).

Crucially, emojis face the problem of racism. The original designs of emojis were heavily biased towards 'white' people in the use of a single skin tone. But a far more significant issue is the fluid meaning of the individual emojis depending on their use, context and the intended recipient. The net result is that while individuals might shirk at writing racist profanities directed towards a public figure such as a sportsperson, they often will not hesitate using a symbol with racist connotations when used in a specific context. Symbols intended to cause offence can include the banana and monkey emojis as well as others that have been employed for their ability to convey analogy for purposes well beyond any original intention. These more prejudiced uses show that technologies can be deployed beyond their original purpose and design, and there is rarely, if ever, a sole use or meaning. The human capacity for applying and understanding polysemy is boundless and can be applied to both good and bad purposes.

Despite the long and exciting history of visual symbols being used to communicate meaning, the endpoint for this chapter's discussion settles on this somewhat more sombre reminder. Management that utilises visual techniques can never fully mature without first recognising this potential for polysemy and then actively working to design out the potential for misinterpretation, misappropriation or just blatant misuse. Multiple meanings might not be readily evident in a pie or radar chart, but in conjunction with the additions of symbols, various colour schemes and written language usage, the prospect still remains. The challenge, or at least one of the many challenges, for visual management is to be self-aware through the application of an ethical and inclusive approach to representation.

3 A theory of visual management

The current use of visual tools, technologies and techniques in management are a disparate collection of actions, processes and thoughts that are waiting for a theory (or theories) of visual management. A theory of visual management necessarily gathers design thinking about contemporary effective communication practices (Hassi and Laakso 2011), the necessity of supporting operational needs, the ways in which the strategic direction of an organisation can be embedded within its culture (Carvalho 2019), and maintaining alignment with vision and mission (Campbell 1992). With this range of interests being represented, a feature of any theory of visual management is its necessarily holistic perspective, its attempt to not silo activities into arbitrary or even incorrect classifications and to represent organisational needs across the short, medium and long term. As outlined earlier, the theorisation presented here is heavily shaped by a material culture understanding of the artefact (Oestigaard 2004). The founding argument to this theorisation is that business documents, whether a report, the description of a process or a corporate dashboard, are all artefacts of the organisation's culture. Contemporary management practices tend towards a messy assemblage of artefacts that are collectively incoherent because they tend to reflect a mix of current and previous 'best' practices found externally rather than genuinely being an echo of the internal organisational culture. Acceptance of

DOI: 10.4324/9781003304166-3

this 'copycat' approach without synthesis or context within the organisation does say something about that internal culture. An artefact-based perspective encourages the development of a critical internal 'language' that is shared and understood across the organisation.

Presented in this way, a visual management approach neatly links to focusing on the strengths and purpose of the organisation and an invocation to purposively do fewer things. Advocacy of this sentiment is a particularly valuable perspective for start-ups and growing organisations, where there is an inevitable tendency for focus to be drawn away from key activities into more regular operational tasks and functions even when people in the organisation possess little or no experience in this way. Great app developers are rarely great accountants or marketers and sometimes the very opposite. One important goal for visual management is to represent the organisation strategically and dynamically 'on a page' in a way that is meaningful to everyone inside as well as those beyond. The purpose of visually representing the organisation externally is not only a marketing activity; it expresses vision and purpose to other organisations who can provide the expertise and capacity that is not found inside – including accountancy and marketing. Communicating in visual terms to another organisation encourages transparency and like-minded affinity where values and stories align.

The business-focused literature that encourages the development of a theory of visual management is wide-ranging and, at times, unexpected. As a form of explanation, a seminal paper on management is usefully cited. While Porter's (1979) Theory of Five Forces is relevant to general business studies, it has a place too in informing visual management. The important linkage is found in the sole visual 'artefact' presented by the paper and which is labelled in this way by the paper itself. Arguably, in this one artefact is communicated the essence – the whole story – of the paper. And this artefact has propelled Porter's paper to occupy a seminal role in the development of management education. Over 7,800 direct citations and potentially a further 72,000 links to other various versions is a significant achievement for any author (scholar.google.com/citations?user=g9WIbh0AAAAJ). Other less well-known works, such as Russell-Jones' (1995) *Management Change Pocketbook,* reveal a perspective on visual management that says any concept should be explainable through the presentation of a single artefact. The increasing and continued popularisation of Osterwalder and Pigneur's (2013) *Business Model Canvas,* with nearly 17,000 citations (scholar.google.com/scholar?cites=1911521120462552255), is another visual artefact that has propelled the approach into mainstream acceptance. Osterwalder and Pigneur's acknowledged synthesis of other models and systems of business model creation found in their book supports the second observation of this chapter's theorisation regarding visual management. An artefact that is external to the organisation is valuable only when it has been adopted and naturalised into its prevailing culture. When the business model canvas is part of a programme to change the prevailing culture (Mauruya 2012), then the emphasis on making it part of the organisation is even more important. In a domestic setting, '"things" act as the embodiment of meaningful social relations and significant connections between family members, friends and even wider social networks' (Money 2007) and there is no reason to suggest that organisations are not one of these wider networks. Despite this observation, very few exemplars of the business model canvas artefact modify the initial design or, for example, deploy images or use emojis in populating the model.

This theorisation supports the adoption of a critical perspective regarding the language and management of organisations (Ahmad and Widén 2018). A further benefit is the way that an attention to artefacts – as proxies to direct human interaction (Fletcher and Greenhill 2007) – further emphasises the role of people within the organisation.

In theorising visual management, the focus is not the wider project of creating an archaeology of business, but more specifically on understanding the material culture of management. Unpacking this statement further, the focus of consideration is the various artefacts that are produced by any organisation and treating them as pivotal to understanding the meaning, purpose, direction and history of that organisation. Without the people of an organisation providing context, insight and narrative, only its artefacts are left to enable understanding of the organisation. Extending this statement, all organisations experience a continuous churn of personnel that removes some knowledge on departure and usually introduces new personnel without prior knowledge of the organisation. The artefacts of the organisation provide the continuity and linkages between past and future. No one is irreplaceable within an organisation, but its artefacts are persistent and this brings a mixture of negative and positive consequences. Organisations become resilient over time through this combination of circumstances – where previous learning and knowledge can become 'stored' in its available artefacts. Making this observation itself is no different for any given cultural group at the wider scale (Ghahramani 2020). A visit to a museum focusing on Victorian policing or prisons is as revealing of the forms of punishment inflicted upon people of a particular culture (or sub-culture) as it is about the development of policing techniques and the criminal justice system (Shore and Johnston 2015).

The example of the museum leads to a further premise found within this discussion. People are generally more visually oriented than textual in how they understand and learn about their environment and situation. The textual descriptions that are presented within a museum are subservient to the primary focus of the exhibit, which is inevitably a form of artefact and a visual reference to the culture being represented. While business may not always recognise the saturated presence of artefacts throughout the organisation, there is a greater vision of this situation found within museological practice. Many museums focus on specific businesses or sectors of the economy, so much so that in the North of England alone there is a silk museum, salt museum, chemistry museum, canal museum, pottery museum, a museum dedicated solely to pencils and a computer museum. In many of the examples, the museum is located within the premises of the former business – the most substantial artefact left by the organisation. Yet the exhibited items at any of these museums primarily focus on the tangible and visual elements of that business, emphasising the sector that it operated within rather than the more common business practices that supported and sustained it over time. Where a specific document is presented publicly, it is often only for its decorative qualities or because it contains a specific reference to an event or individual of note. The many more documents associated with these businesses that are held by the museum sit away from public view in storage and are only available to researchers on request. The opportunity to visit a museum of accounting or human resources remains confined to individual virtual offerings. There are two conclusions that can be drawn from this situation. Visually oriented artefacts have more impact for the purpose of education, entertainment and cultural heritage and by extension, this applies to the world of work too, particularly if all forms of work are considered an aspect of knowledge exchange. From an organisational point of view, the activities represented solely by textual documents in these museums, as well as in ongoing businesses, are particularly susceptible to digitalisation and automation. These are the items hidden away from sight in the industrial museum and the elements of the lowest value knowledge exchange. These things are the most routine of tasks within the organisation and they are tasks repeated with little variation between organisations.

The mundane operational tasks of organisations regularly represented in textual artefacts are those most prone to automation and this is one of the changes that is accelerated through digital transformation. Systematic technological change will shift these types of actions from something undertaken by people using text-based tools to a point where the actions are undertaken automatically and visually reported to people. 'People' in the previous sentence may currently be interpreted as 'worker' and 'manager'. If digital transformation is to be a positive social and economic force then it could be argued that the ongoing realignment of roles would move the 'worker' into the role of a 'manager' – specifically of knowledge and technology (Young et al. 2021). A less positive view of this process may see the 'worker' just displaced sideways into the same role with another organisation or worse into unemployment (Acemoglu and Restrepo 2018).

With Osterwalder and Pigneur's (2013) visual arrangement – and simplification – of the business model, more strategic aspects of the organisation can be explored for consolidation into a regularised pattern. Their later work on the value proposition of an organisation (2014) takes strategizing in an organisation to another level of shared commonality. Working with this single guiding tool based on the collective knowledge of many experts ensures that many organisations now know the gains and pains of their customers and have defined their own 'gain creators' and 'pain relievers'. What becomes important in response to a VUCA world that offers insights regarding best practice is the need for genuine coherent organisational distinctiveness. This statement does not solely describe strategic difference, which hovers conceptually between the poles of operations and tactics and that of vision and values. The need is one that draws on organisational culture and its material culture. A statement that acknowledges the sentiment of the famous quote apocryphally linked to Drucker, that 'culture eats strategy', (Engel 2018). This introduces an implied extension of the Cultural Web model (Johnson and Scholes 1993) which is arguably blind to the influence of artefacts as powerful proxies to direct human action (Fletcher and Greenhill 2007).

Applying a material culture perspective to the output of management within an organisation is a personal frustration with the conventional representation of strategy as well as more operational details. Despite actively voicing these frustrations, it is very difficult to escape the flatland presented by lengthy text-based documents. Strategies are management documents created with an intention to last. From personal experience, strategic positioning statements, strategy documents and action plans tend to be most read at a point of time closest to their creation with the readership then dropping off rapidly across the life of the strategy. Finding this pattern of use is not an indicator of any rapid assimilation into organisational culture. As an artefact, this type of strategy has a far more limited lifespan than is intended. A rising or even flat graph of readership over time would be more indicative of its acceptance and the active use of a strategy. Having this more desirable pattern of organisational behaviour would indicate that these documents were continuously being accessed across an organisation, being referred to by managers and being shared as a guide to others regarding the change occurring within the organisation. In a more positive scenario, the treatment of the strategy as a useful tool would make it an effective artefact of management.

The challenge is multiple. Strategic documents should contain vital details, but these details are often buried in amongst other material of less relevance for any given audience or describe mundane operations or the systematised aspects of the strategy already captured in visual material such as the business model canvas. The consequence is that focus is distracted away from distinctiveness by describing what a strategy is in its conceptualisation rather than what the organisation will be specifically doing with this concept. It is a core critique of the way strategy creation is undertaken in organisations. The value of taking a visual approach is to emphasise the specific strategic undertaking and the distinctiveness it creates rather than reiterating existing knowledge, journaling senior management speculations or documenting common organisational practice. The risk is that a strategy becomes a description of repetitive actions – that can in some way may be automated – or a vision – that is far removed from any everyday experience. An analogy would be for an artist tasked with restoring the Sistine Chapel ceiling to focus on describing the scaffolding, brushes and drop-sheets they will be using and then how extraordinary the end result will be rather than explaining how they will match the colours or their own technique for applying the paint.

Strategy and other 'big picture' documents of this type suffer from the existential issue of presenting unknown unknowns to its intended audiences. The audience does not necessarily know what to seek out within the document to find the things that are of the most relevance. The larger and more wide-ranging the document, the more comprehensive its contents, but then the bigger the document, the less likely it will be read in full by anyone ever beyond the original authors. Sitting in strategic planning meetings where the mantra for the delivered outcome is that it will be a 'living document' often signals the death knell for that same document. These observations prompt the question: why is it so?

An analogy can be drawn with the PhD process. In this process, an individual will spend at least three years working diligently on a lengthy piece of research that will be highly specialised, focused and consequently have a very limited potential audience in its final form. Even those lucky enough to publish some part of their PhD will often find themselves editing out significant chunks of the work that would be considered less appealing to a broader audience. The elements of a PhD usually discarded prior to publication are the most commonly presented materials, large elements of the methodology – the most operational details – the parts that focus on the thinking about thinking – the philosophy and vision of the work. For those familiar with the 'research onion' (Saunders et al. 2015), it is both a simultaneous skinning and a de-coring of the core artefact presented in this work. And even with this editing in place, the audience for most articles or monographs based upon a PhD remains finite if not incredibly small. There is no intended criticism of the PhD process itself in this statement (because the process is at least as important as the final output), but rather a reflection of the complex issues of conveying meaning to any audience through a single document. Strategy documents and other documents suffer the same problem as a PhD. As the document must inevitably address multiple audiences, the likelihood of any given part of the document being relevant to any specific audience diminishes rapidly. Organisations that do attempt to tackle this challenge find the most viable solution is to take the key points and represent them either as bullet points or through concise information graphics.

The 'translation' solution is a workaround to a recognisable and common problem. Attempting to create a 'living document' by adding visual elements to a long text-based document avoids addressing the real issue. If the focus of attention for the intended audiences will be on the information graphics and the summary bullet points, what purpose remains for the text of the document? An exception might be some form of evidence that supports the representation offered by more accessible and digestible artefacts. The solution to the problem mirrors the innovation and transformation achieved during the development of proto-Sumerian. The realisation that the action of baking tokens into clay pillows was no longer required if the markings on the outside already indicated the same information follows the same thought process. If the information graphics, summary points, graphs and images reflect the textual information in a document, there is no longer need for that text. Tufte (1983) offers a similar observation in more florid terms: 'For non-data-ink, less is more. For data-ink, less is a bore.' With increasingly data-driven (Mandinach et al. 2006) or data-informed (Wang 2020) management the process of creating strategies and other forms of organisational documentation is a translational step from the available data through a textual description and narrative onwards to a visual representation of that narrative (Figure 3.1). If the suitable tools and people are available to receive

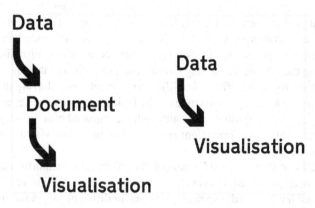

Figure 3.1 From data to 'living' visualisation

data and directly apply interpretation to that data and then finally represent the interpretation through some form of visualisation, the role and purpose of the intermediate documentation step becomes more questionable.

This is at the core of an artefact-based interpretation of management material culture and one solution to the creation of coherent organisational distinctiveness. If the various documents and visualisations and even the data itself all tell the same story in slightly different ways, then there is no need to provide a written description, except for the audience whose preference is a written description. The challenge of multiple audiences having multiple and varying needs is complex. Some of these needs are focused on delivering a specific action around an individual function, some have a dominant learning style through the use of written materials, while for others it is personal preference. Personal preference is important and should not be discounted. A text-based format may be a necessity for some needs, but it is one that can be accommodated and does not necessitate that the starting point for management communication is document-based. Preferences based only on prior practice combined with personal reluctance for anything new is a key barrier to transformative change in any organisation.

The other aspect of creating coherent organisational distinctiveness is FUSY. It relates to how the artefacts that are being created connect to the living organisational culture that they represent. The relationship is two-way. Any artefact produced by the organisational culture should echo a common shared language, mutual understanding and encapsulate the vision – the yearning – of the organisation to progress. There is the need to be flexible too. The visual language of the organisation needs to change, evolve and be able to express the organisational response to a changeable VUCA world.

The components to create a visual language for management lay scattered around and are freely accessible. There are already examples of theoretical and strategic visualisations that have become commonplace and heavily used within management that rely heavily on the simplicity of the visualisation rather than nuance, accuracy or precision regarding the underlying data. The popularity of the two-by-two square matrix in various visualisations, including the Boston Consulting Group (BCG) Matrix and the Johari Window, points to the benefit of simplified representations as having the most appeal within a management context. The Unicode character set even offers this 2 × 2 grid as a symbol – ⊞ – although the 'squared plus' is intended to represent addition-like operations as well as having a close visual similarity with the Windows logo.

The case of Porter's Five Forces (1979) and its continued influence have already been presented. However, the popularity goes still further. The diagram itself has been redrawn multiple times for different papers for different purposes and by a range of different authors from undergraduates through to research professors. The general concept embedded in the diagram is itself useful for representing the convergence of multiple variables and has been used in this way to describe different phenomena beyond those originally intended by Porter.

The re-usage and re-purposing of visual symbols introduce a further challenge to visual management as a system for creating coherent management artefacts in an organisation. The use of theorised literature is certainly appropriate and commendable within any organisation, but a coherent visual language – as part of the coherent organisational distinctiveness – brings the need for localised and contextualised purpose. Porter's Five Forces is a theorised and generalised representation of the interlocking challenges facing an organisation from the outside world. What can be detached from this specific use, as well as other similar management visualisation devices, is its integration into a visual language for that organisation itself. A visual language is not just a discussion of stylistic difference, but rather how the current balance of understanding and yearning within the organisation is shown through its use of visual elements. The stylistic considerations are readily solved through digital technologies that can change visual features through Cascading Style Sheets (CSS) or through an interface that offers total customisation. The Noun Project provides a customisation feature to its subscribers that enables them to change the colour, size and other features of the individual symbols to suit the stylistic preferences of an organization's visual language. But integration with an organisation's culture is a more significant challenge. Addressing the challenge begins with acknowledgement that such a thing even exists beyond the scope of colour, size, font or stroke width. It is a case of recognising that a visual language goes beyond the scope of a brand or branding and enters the realm of capturing the focus and essence of the underlying organisational culture.

However, it is the organisations with existing strong brand awareness that are those most likely to understand the value of a visual language that extends across the entire organisation's purpose and actions. The example of IKEA is a case in point (Fager n.d.). The use of visual language across IKEA's consumer presence shows the strength of thinking contained within its brand. The fact that it is a multinational company with origins in a non-English-speaking country gives even greater imperative to maintaining clear internal thinking about how it communicates. The result can be seen in artefacts that might be regarded as mundane, such as the instructions necessary for constructing its flat pack furniture. IKEA's functional communications with its customers can be done without any words and solely using visual diagrams that are consistent in their approach from one piece of furniture to the next. A particular feature of note in IKEA communications is the presence of a human dimension. Figures of people are included to provide a sense of scale as well as a warning when lifting an item that it may require two people or when a call to the helpdesk might be appropriate. Evidence of this visual language can be seen across IKEA properties and extends beyond furniture to include its food offerings and the way it represents internal signage in its stores. Arguably, the attempt to reduce the number of different types of fixtures in flat pack furniture is further acknowledgement of the value associated with having a consistent visual language. Providing a small set of different fastenings for a wide range of furnishings is clearly efficient economically, makes good business sense and it does mean there is less chance for the misinterpretation of the instructions or the prospect of using the wrong fitting in the wrong place. Making an organisational commitment to continuous change has created additional value for IKEA furniture in that individual items can be reconfigured beyond the existing instructions and original purpose attributed to them by the company itself. IKEA furniture can be manipulated, altered and hacked to create new types of furniture purposes or styles by the owners of the furniture rather than being limited by the manufacturer's intentions. Having flexibility around the outcomes and the multi-function capability of components has created an online community of IKEA hackers. Individual examples of owner ingenuity can be routinely found on social media channels, such as Pinterest. In this way IKEA furniture items almost hold an inherent value as a tool in that they are multi-functional and adaptable – even if these features are rarely explored by individual owners.

Another familiar global brand that shares many of the qualities in its own visual language with that of IKEA is LEGO. There are many parallels. Originating in a Scandinavian country and working with people with varying literacy skills, in this case young children, shows similar priorities for creating a visual language across the entire organisation. LEGO by design is intended to be used in infinite combinations. However, LEGO's renaissance as an influential global brand over the last 20 years has come from sustained enthusiasm for specific kits that produce familiar items built out of Lego bricks. These kits are all supplied in the same way as IKEA furniture with instructions that utilise no words and rely entirely upon visual imagery. One of the key attributes of both Ikea and LEGO instructions is that where a piece has a requirement for degree of precision in terms of its length, the instructions will print the exact length of that item in the instructions so that someone building the model can physically align the right piece against the image in the instructions to ensure that they are using the correct piece. For LEGO, despite the popularity of kits that have specific outcomes, the core LEGO principle of reuse remains. Even the most unusually shaped LEGO brick will always be able to be utilised in new and unexpected ways in a new construction because the connection principles of all Lego bricks remain consistent irrespective of the specific design challenges this might bring to creating the individual model. The LEGO experience offers a lesson for management. In the restricted syntax of LEGO, no one is disappointed when their kit contains some four-by-two rectilinear bricks (the original and standard brick dimensions) if they suit the need that exists in the model. The experience of a LEGO user's modelling experience in acknowledging the role of each block within the overall model echoes the value of deploying existing models and tools drawn from the VUCA world into a business – but only if they correctly fit the need within the overall organisational purpose.

LEGO shows the way in which a strong visual language can translate to different contexts. LEGO has become an important game franchise on platforms such as Microsoft's Xbox and Sony's PlayStation and has worked with companies such as Minecraft – now owned by Microsoft – in a form of retrospective re-engineering to engage with effectively the LEGO equivalent of an online world. As a result, it is possible to play in the virtual LEGO playground of Minecraft. Minecraft's popularity has helped reinvigorate the LEGO brand. Now it is possible to purchase LEGO kits that physically model the virtual Minecraft world. As a result, the tangible visual language of LEGO has reconnected with itself through the intermediary influence of a digital twin.

Other organisations are conscious of their visual language in ways that extend beyond brand image or generating content. Taking the purpose of visual management beyond marketing actions is a key step in the movement towards being a truly mature organisation and beyond being just visually oriented. A visually managed organisation takes the artefacts that it creates and sees them as central to the operations and organisation of the business itself. Visually oriented businesses may well be on the way to being visually managed, but their focus is on the external representation of the organisation to an audience that is short on attention span and suffering from information overload. Placing importance on the artefacts of the organisation is one thing, but recognising that some of these artefacts can be tools for future use in new and different ways is a further level of maturity that few organisations can claim. Published as a limited edition in 2015, the Feltron annual report is a rare example of a business report built from the starting perspective of a visual language to convey its key purpose and points – in this case, an assessment of the current state of art in self-tracking technologies (feltron.com/FAR14.html).

Visual management in an organisation emerges from the narrower fields of branding and content creation and takes up the wider challenge of bringing the entire organisation together as a single entity. If the artefacts of an organisation are its central defining things that are available for internal and external scrutiny, then the value of these artefacts approaches that of being a tool. With this observation, the information systems perspective is introduced. The artefacts of the organisation are its tools. These tools have a clear purpose to bring the six elements of the system – the organisation – together in a well-connected way (Figure 3.2). An organisation uses its artefacts to bring together the components of communication and processes, as well as its people, into connection with its hardware, software and data. The use of reporting tools to visualise the data held by the organisation is an obvious example of integration using visual management techniques, but the value of this approach can be identified elsewhere too. In a people context, visualisations are the tools of knowledge management. Knowledge management is a crucial issue for organisations, especially given the post-COVID impact of high staff churn (Harris 2021). Existing artefacts are not often considered for their role in the context of shaping knowledge management. What we see within an organisation shapes what we think of that organisation. What we think of the organisation shapes how we communicate about

Figure 3.2 Components of the system

that organisation, both internally and externally. These internal cycles of communication then return as the artefacts of the organisation and repeat the cycle (Figure 3.3).

The processes of an organisation are tied to the use of visual or textual artefacts too. The processes of an organisation are themselves artefacts. Each process is a proxy for the ways of working and perspectives of some people who were in the organisation previously as well as currently. The processes are the embedded wisdom of these people and echo back the culture of that organisation at a particular point in time. In this way, current people and the legacy of previous people are the challenges that organisational culture presents for projects of strategic change. Changing one process involves changing a small aspect of culture. Each process is developed for a specific purpose and with a defined intention. The tendency, however, is that as a tool, it will later be adapted by people to serve ever-evolving purposes. The challenge for people within an organisation is to understand the relevance of the process (or the tool more generally) and how it relates

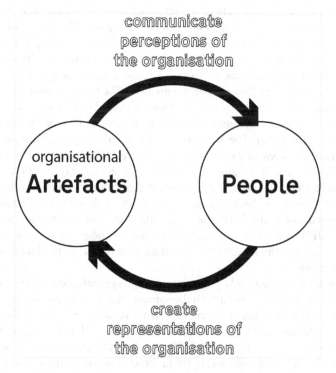

Figure 3.3 Artefacts and the culture/communications loop

to their own needs. The scale of this challenge is compounded when the processes are experienced by people who are external to the organisation. In this first point of interaction with the organisation is the telling indicator of its underlying internal culture. As one example, a local bakery that produces a variety of fresh goods has a specific process for online ordering. Ordering must be done two days in advance of the collection of the baked goods. Only collection is possible and online ordering is only possible between 9:30am and 11:30am on three days of the week. To compound these restrictions, the system is designed to empty the online shopping cart after eight minutes if the order has not been completed. Such a very unexpected way of approaching ecommerce highlights a particular organisational culture, but it is one that does not stop customers queuing outside the shop before it opens. The intersection of such a varied range of experiences would map somewhat curiously against Osterwalder and Pigneur's Value Proposition Canvas (Osterwalder et al. 2014) in terms of the balance of pains and gains customers find when interacting with this successful business. The bread is very good.

The software element of a system is particularly significant for deploying visual management. It is firmly within the software element of the organisation that the visual artefacts of the organisation are generated in combination with its people. It is within this locus of the manufacture of artefacts that is reinforced by the fact that software itself is not culturally neutral. Software transports the meanings, values and perspectives of its original designers. Like processes, software contains a stored proxy of previous human actions – its creators and maintainers. The hidden human presence in software is reinforced by the sentiment expressed by Conway's Law that organisations design systems that mirror their own communication structure (Bailey et al. 2013). The subjective and cultural role of software within an organisation remains relatively unconsidered within academia (Fletcher 2020) and yet it is a significant influence in shaping organisational perspectives and behaviours. Recognition of this influence tends to come out only in the general discussion of organisations in the context of addiction to social media channels (Marino et al. 2020) or cybersecurity risk (Malatji et al. 2019). But software shapes the thinking of people across the organisation and that thinking then shapes the artefacts that are produced by the organisation.

The artefacts produced by the software of an organisation are crucial for visual management. It is through the software that the linkage of the organisation's data to its people is created. What is important is not only what data is held and what can be collected, but also what should be represented and how it should be represented. The problem of representation is located between people and software, not data. Process and communication play a role too. It is almost a cliché that 'data is the new oil' and the purpose of the statement is to emphasise the value of data in the organisation. The analogy works on another level to recognise that data in isolation, without refinement, provides no value to an organisation. It's only through the mediation of the other elements of the system that data comes to have any value or meaning for the organisation – as it is refined into insight through a combination of software and processes that are controlled and directed by people.

Perhaps most challenging of all the relationships in the system is the relationship of the hardware of an organisation. Hardware is not just the physical computer technology that is physically represented by a computer, but the vast array of physical equipment and buildings that encompass all the tangible things associated with that organisation. From a consumer's point of view, the hardware is closely tied to the branding of the organisation. For example, the layout of a McDonald's restaurant and its ordering system represent the entirety of the organisation. Changes to the hardware of an organisation shape the way people interact and behave in relation to that organisation. The McDonald's example is indicative. McDonald's has changed from its earliest incarnation as a fast-food outlet with heavy use of plastic and industrial fittings to a more ecologically aware organisation with wooden fixtures and a preference for a green colour scheme that has no clowns in sight (McDonald's n.d.). A vision of this type changes the representation of McDonald's from a fast-food takeaway to a restaurant and echoes the current underlying 'Accelerating the Arches' strategy. The hardware of an organisation itself is difficult to shape around a coherent visual distinctiveness unless the degree of control that is exerted centrally is significant. Franchised-based operations such as McDonald's have this capability. Another way that hardware can be embedded in the visual language of an organisation can be seen in the modernist architectural trend for functional transparency. The Pompidou Centre in Paris and the Lloyd's of London building hallmark this approach. Functional transparency could be described as the physical manifestation of Tufte's (1983) call to maximise data-ink. Although Goldfinger may now be reified in the same way as Rogers, his Brutalist work for the Greater London Council better voices the language of his employer. Trellick and Balfron Towers emphasise the lift shaft and its connections to these high-rise concrete residences (Figure 3.4). The towers are a response to rising populations in post-war Britain that put into reality the elegant but controversial functionalist design philosophy of Le Corbusier by creating 'machines for living' (Cohen 2004). Brutalism is itself a punning reference to Le Corbusier's original phrase 'beton brut' – raw concrete – emphasising a commitment to design transparency by revealing the construction materials being used (Altun 2016). The University of Essex makes a direct linkage between its original brutalist buildings and the vision expressed at its foundation in the 1960s for innovation

Figure 3.4 The hardware representing the language of the post-war Greater London
Council

(Source: photographer Ethan Nunn, https://creativecommons.org/licenses/by-sa/4.0/deed.en)

and doing things differently (www.essex.ac.uk/about/our-history). Smaller organisations, organisations with less direction from a central authority or a less theorised approach will be challenged by these ways of producing a consistent physical and visual language within its hardware.

Hardware – in the most physical and general sense of the term – is important, but organisations now realise that printed documents such as the annual report sit anachronistically with a digital world. With real-time data being generated and available continuously, there is a clear rationale to deliver a more continuous form of reporting that can mirror the purpose of the traditional annual report while having greater currency and immediacy in a faster-paced world. Taking this line of thinking leads to specific forms of digital transformation and organisational change as well encouraging the rise of corporate dashboards.

4 The current state of play in visual management (and the tyranny of corporate dashboards)

There is significant evidence for the current use of visual management tools and techniques across a wide range of organisations. The advance of a range of literature about corporate dashboards (Skorka 2017), the elegant presentation of data (McCandless 2014) and even the use of emojis in corporate communications (Alshenqeeti 2016; Gilles Doiron 2018) all populate the library of visual management. Similarly, academic literature makes regular use of explanatory diagrams that encapsulate core concepts in a single image (e.g. Gibbs Cycle of Reflection 1988). Taking this visual approach even further, there are an increasing number of high-profile and impactful journals that ask for a visual abstract with submissions from authors (www.elsevier.com/authors/tools-and-resources/visual-abstract) or offer opportunities to create cartoon abstracts (authorservices.taylorandfrancis.com/cartoon-abstracts/). All these examples show the beneficial value of visual artefacts to improve understanding among an audience.

What is generally lacking in these approaches is an underlying and integrating approach to visual management. Not only is this a lack of a theorised visionary approach (Chapter 3), but it is more simply a lack of consistency. Even within academic literature there is no common visual language beyond the patterns of quantitative data representation such as a bar chart and qualitative data such as a circle with clockwise arrows (used by Gibbs). Scholarly journals rely on the visual representations offered by individual authors

DOI: 10.4324/9781003304166-4

without imposing any standard format or style (and arguably rightly so). Equally, authors contributing to a journal are generally not visually inspired by work presented in previous articles from the same journal even when they cite these works to make the intellectual linkage. While journals may rightly represent a cross-section of different authorial visual approaches, it is more concerning that there is often no consistency in the visual language employed by the same author across multiple papers (a confession of my own guilt in this regard).

A lack of consistent or theorised approaches to the use of visual communications in an organisational context is evident for the same reasons as personal ones. Superficially, evidence of this lack of stability can be seen in the differences between an organisation's external communications and how it interacts with its employees as one potential benchmark. Another indicator is the high word counts used in the planning processes of an organisation. Verbose documents that are read once and rarely referred to again hint at issues within the organisation's culture – in the same way that all artefacts reveal something about the culture that created them. Long documents that are needed to explain everything suggest poor day-to-day sharing of knowledge, a lack of management transparency and an uncertainty about the intended audience or a general failure to understand the audience. Verbosity in documents sometimes indicates the need for the author to journal their own thought processes so they can move to a more critical and strategic view. In a less mature or smaller organisation, some journaling activity may be a necessary part of the reading/ writing process of learning for an individual manager but does not need to be shared as part of organisational planning and strategy.

The use of large documents in an organisation can work. Haphazard examples of success with this approach show that the key points of a wordy plan can be absorbed into an organisational culture, but further widespread engagement directly with a plan of this type is largely symbolic. The routes that let this dissemination occur are an exploration of how the four different forms of learning could hypothetically interact between the layers of organisational context (Figure 4.1) or between the contentious claim (Rudolph et al. 2018) for generational differences towards working (Jones 2018) (Figure 4.2). The approach acknowledges the critiques regarding the validity of an overly tight classification of learning styles (Pashler 2008). A visual management approach promotes the primary use of a symbolic layer through visual artefacts that strip back visionary and strategic planning to its key critical (and communicative) meanings. Making the key points about the big picture in the right way across a range of audiences (e.g. learning styles and generations) gives time and space to link this thinking with the day-to-day reality and activities of the organisation.

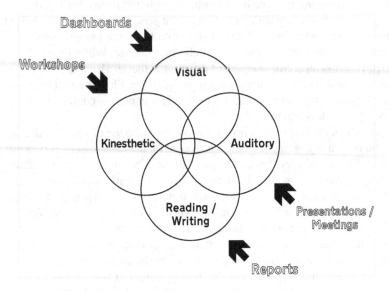

Figure 4.1 Linking the four learning styles with internal actions and artefacts – with unrealised opportunities in the overlaps

Figure 4.2 Linking different generation perspectives within the organisation (a tentative differentiation that excludes the earlier Baby Boomers)

Corporate dashboards, at least in their current manifestation, deserve specific attention in terms of their relationship to a broader vision of visual management and to the ways that they currently represent the organisation. Dashboards extract specific measurable outputs during the reporting phase of management. For already quantitative aspects of organisational performance such as financials, these are directly visualised. More qualitative aspects, including culture, are represented through proxy measures such as churn rate or the proportions of employees undertaking a mandatory training activity. Most dashboards, however, do not enable direct input routes back into further organisational planning and learning (Figure 1.2). The visualisations are one-way in their function and isolated from the other reported metrics. With a little imagination, it is possible to envisage an interface in which dragging visual elements in a report could support decision-making and forward planning by presenting the resultant scenario that becomes possible through an alteration of the variables represented by the elements. It could become a form of game-like interface that is an integrated business tool (Chapter 8 discusses this possibility further). Developing a system that links reporting and planning requires the technical capability for the reporting mechanism to retain the relational context that it has to other variables that are being presented, as well as linking the underlying meaning of the final presented variable back into the operations of the organisation. Functionality of this type is already presented through the wide range of management education simulations, where decision-making and the playing out of scenarios is a key form of hands-on kinesthetic learning for university and college students. However, many of these simulations rely primarily on a text-based interface to input specific values or to select from a list of options. A more complete and 'live' example of this possibility is CyberSyn. The Project CyberSyn experiment in the early 1970s initiated by Stafford Beer at the request of the Chilean government is an early example of how this speculative interactive dashboard may function (Espejo 2014). Built in a different political era, the project utilised the technology of the time, including teletext machines, to attempt to direct the nationalised elements of Chile's economy. The system worked by linking a single strategic centre with its operational spokes. The centre would receive reports from government-owned farms and in response instructions would be sent back based on the prevailing overall conditions relating to the cost of raw materials, weather projections and the projected sales price of different crops. The success of the project was never evaluated, as the government lost power to Pinochet in a military coup. The scale of the CyberSyn vision from 50 years ago somewhat diminishes the apparent ambition of current corporate dashboards. A mature visual management tool, rather than 'just' visual reporting, links 'seeing' different views of the organisation with the kinesthetic actions needed to realise its vision, including decision-making and the setting of targets.

Describing the current situation of visual management is more often done in terms of marketing-focused, external or even superficial values. As with many aspects of organisations as they navigate their way through the challenges and opportunities brought by digitalisation, anything prefaced by 'digital' is generally representative of an early phase in the adoption and integration of the technology into the core of an organisation. Evidence of this phenomenon can be seen in activities such as digital marketing and even digital transformation. The fact that digital marketing was the first function in business to fully embrace digitalisation is not surprising. As the most externally facing of business functions, the capabilities of digital technologies that were made available with the evolution of the World Wide Web are closely aligned with the needs and purpose of the marketing function. The net result is that most organisations of any size or scale now have well-developed digital marketing operations. The digitalisation of activity is so central to marketing that working without it is now the anomaly. Without digital technology, the marketing function for most businesses would almost certainly be ineffective. The maturity of digital marketing creates its own challenges in relation to the argument being presented here. Senior management in an organisation can erroneously come to a position that equates having a fully digitalised marketing function with being a fully digital business and having a high level of organisational digital maturity. A line of thinking that follows this logic diminishes and discredits the benefits of further, wider digital transformation and would dismiss the role visual management could play.

Similar observations can be made for developments undertaken in the name of digital transformation. While digital transformation reaches further into the functions and operations of an organisation than marketing, its label often hides the fact that there is significant internal change occurring in the organisation that reaches far beyond the implementation of any specific digital technology or process. The era of (digital) transformation brings the relationship of data and the software that manipulates it into closer alignment with the people of the organisation. Digital transformation is possible because of the accelerated and attenuated capabilities that digital tools bring but the transformation that it initiates is experienced across the whole organisation (Fenton et al. 2020). Whereas the focus of marketing was on the external environment, digital transformation brings a need for people inside the organisation to change. The automation of processes reduces the need for direct human action within routine functions and enables people to be released for more complex and subjective aspects of an organisation's management. Robotic processes combined with artificial intelligence can remove the need for routine decision-making (Jarrahi 2018). Human input is still needed in these circumstances for the one-in-a-million exception and to ensure that rules-based processes continue to adhere to the ethical alignment and overall vision of the organisation.

The current situation for visual management follows these two earlier phenomena. There is reliance on the available digital tools (software), the people who can communicate with these tools and the existing data to display the far-ranging and deep insights possible through visual communications. Current visualisation processes rely on specialist people with a combination of graphic design skills and the ability to manipulate and interpret complex datasets. These are the transformers that Neurath (Neurath and Kinross 2009) envisaged. They are highly skilled operators of specific tools who can produce the desired outcomes for an organisation – data scientists, graphic designers, and programmers. However, this occurs only in organisations that have the foresight, investment and capability to recognise and deploy people with these types of skills in their communications and regard this work as a central tenet of the vision. While it is a tentative hierarchy of maturity, the relationship between those who have visualisation skills and access to visualisation tools represents the initial defining stage in what is a longer-term development for organisations. Without diminishing the value or purpose of graphic designers or data scientists, the overall maturity of an organisation in relation to visual management will only develop when a wider range of people are able to communicate through visual artefacts using tools that are relatively familiar and commonplace and that require fewer specialist skills to use successfully (Figure 4.3). At the core of this statement is not an argument for training more graphic designers, but rather one that all students should be more conscious of the value of visual representations and visualisation within the organisations that they enter as young graduates. The types of changes seen in the practices of digital marketing and processes of digital transformation within organisations have become increasingly visible as a new generation of workers enter the world of work and apply their own point of view and ways of working. The change

Figure 4.3 Visual management maturity in an organisation

has been hallmarked with the coming of Gen Z workers (Pichler et al. 2021) but it is a pattern of systemic change that can be identified in all recent generations as they enter their professional working lives as new recruits with the ambition and intention to make a difference from their predecessors. Identifying this attitude for change as being present in all new generations of workers challenges much of the rhetoric about the impact and experience of Generation Z entering the world of work (Rudolph et al. 2018).

The role of new people as change agents within an organisation introduces another component in identifying the maturity of an organisation and its preparedness for visual management. The basis of this indicator rests in the relationship between people and the organisation's data. An information systems perspective acknowledges this necessary linkage, but maturity around the management of the organisation through visual means requires that people understand the role of visualisation as a way of taking data and expressing it in a way that is both accessible and meaningful to all its people. A relationship of this form relates well to previous literature that has already discussed the value and benefits of well-presented data through visual means. There is a linkage in this observation with the need to recognise the presence of different learning styles – or styles of knowledge exchange – in an organisation and the primacy of reading (writing). Both Tufte's (1983, 1990, 2006a) and McCandless's (2012, 2014, 2021) work express the need for information to be conveyed in elegant, simple and ultimately beautiful forms. While these earlier works talk about individual items, there is less attention given to the creation of an organisational language and what would be described in material culture terms as a coherent assemblage of artefacts. At the same time, consciously avoiding the prescriptive imposition of a fully formed language presents a narrow path between too little and too much prescription regarding communication practices. The need is to rebalance organisational preference onto visual rather than written expression and not the wholesale reinvention of the language of business. The experience of Blissymbolics (1978) and emojis as well as natural human language development show the need for individual flexibility based around a stability of core meaning that is mutually comprehensible and some internal need or a cultural yearning for this change. The FUSY acronym again.

This cautionary warning suggests that any move to visual management is evolutionary rather than revolutionary in its implementation. The lack of an internal visual language in so many organisations is not something that can be altered simply with the switch of corporate focus or a managerial diktat. Internally switching from textually heavy forms of communication and processes is difficult. Making this observation is thoroughly unsurprising and it is not a criticism of the organisations themselves. Patterns of behaviour, what we learn to do, the way we prefer to communicate and how we are trained from a young age stay with us for the remainder of our lives. It is a core tenet of the notion of culture as well as the reason why differences between Generations X, Y and Z are often defined by their preferred forms of instant and personal communication (Jones 2018). It has already been noted that organisational culture embeds the thoughts and actions of previous generations of employees within its artefacts. And, seemingly, the irony of this embedded rootedness to text is expressed by this book itself – as an artefact – which advocates for a visual approach to communications within organisations, yet its thesis is expressed through a lengthy text. In defence of this textually based approach, any more visually oriented presentation could be argued as a form of preaching to the choir. As some form of mitigation to this inevitable challenge, the argument presented here is a consciously 'short form' approach that is punctuated with figures throughout.

There are already many existing signposts to the way in which an organisational culture may evolve towards a preference for visual communication. Any organisation where internal WhatsApp groups flourish sees the increasingly prevalent use of emojis within those communications to succinctly express the variety of emotions related to engagement with that organisation. These modest first steps show the way in which a visual language can be the product of the organisational culture as much as it is a management technique or desire. What is an organisation to do with this conundrum of wanting organisational culture to adopt more visual forms of communication? Hints can be elicited from previous forms of visual management. The tools for the job necessary to express the language itself must be available across the organisational culture (Figure 4.3). Without this ability to access the tools, there is, at the very least, inequality within that organisational culture and potentially worse. As Generation Z workers (Jones 2018) expect their employer's ethics to align with their own values, any lack is anathema. A language that is exclusively the language of management can produce an active resistance to the culture that this hierarchy encourages. Evidence for this can be drawn directly from history, when literacy levels varied between different classes of people (Gatto 2005). Business once relied upon arrays of low-paid staff – usually women – in typing pools to produce communications for dissemination. Such an unequal and hierarchical relationship within early modern business prompted the development of its own phonographic representation of the English language through Pitman shorthand as well as other competing systems, including Gregg, Teeline and Duployan. Pitman is a written system that requires its own specific tools – specifically the ability to produce thin and thick lines (Rabina 2013). Shorthand systems are the written language of the worker – and a specific class of worker – that could not be understood by employers or managers but were necessary for them to produce the final version of communication that was then taken to be authoritative across the business. From this point of view, any revolution in the early 20th century organisation was going to be communicated through shorthand, not the typewritten page. Fans of the 1980 film, *9 to 5*, will recognise the satirical form of this revolution within its storyline. The specificity and limited wider value of these shorthand systems are revealed by the relative lack of adoption into the Unicode system (Unicode.org). Only the Duployan system has been included since 2014, but in contrast, emojis were first included as part of Unicode Version 9 in 2010.

In 21st century organisational terms, there is a preference towards having workers whose engagement is more than transactional. While workers do not expect equivalent status with their bosses, it would now be an unusual situation to use tools for communication internally that are not available to all its workers or channels of communication that are not two-way by design. Even broadcast-style communication tools are available to all workers – even if not all workers will use them. The 'all staff' email list, the organisation-wide Yammer channel and @everyone in Slack are all examples of these available channels. Restricting who can access these types of channels or offering different tools for different levels of workers prevents the creation of a single integrating language for the organisation. In an era when digital transformation is having a profound effect upon the perspective organisations have towards their own workers (and vice versa) and especially around the need to become more transparent and open, this idea of creating multiple dialects of interaction within an organisation is simply antithetical.

Stepping back from this discussion, it can be argued that the tool of a pencil provides this desirable common ground to create a single organisational visual language. A tool that encourages creativity and the expression of ideas in a free and flowing way (Fisher 2021). However, the introduction of processes of digitalisation into most organisations means that the aggregation of data required to communicate the underlying activities of an organisation requires more sophisticated tools. What is required is the equivalent of a digitalised pencil. A tool that is easily picked up by anyone in the organisation and empowers them to be expressive with the organisation's entire accessible data. It is an evocative image that many software vendors will claim is already accessible through their own product offering for the right license fee (beta products such whatifi.io; boardview. io; litmaps.co). Systems that show this type of promise have gained recent popularity, such as Notion (notion.so). The many additions that are being developed for the system point to an online organisational environment where sound, video, images and text all sit side-by-side in a way that defies singular classification. It is simultaneously wiki, notes, to-do lists and communications. Notion consultants are already available who can even guide an organisation to be more productive with the system. However, the 'digitalised pencil' will invariably be more mundane and will incorporate already freely available tools for communication. For example, the extensive range of Unicode symbols (unicode.org/charts) that go beyond the standard scripts of existing languages and offer potential for creativity in output and expression but are not bound to existing organisational perspectives or systems.

The creation of a visual language for any organisation and its challenges is a visible representation of the tension between representing quantitative data in combination with the qualitative elements of an organisation. In many circumstances, it is the qualitative elements that define the essential distinguishing elements of one organisation in a sector from another. Examples can be drawn from the UK retail landscape in attempting to define what is different between Aldi and Lidl or Tesco and ASDA. The recent introduction into UK higher education of what is described as the Proceed metric shows a similar tension between the quantitative data and the specific quality of a course experience (Office for Students 2021). With this new metric designed by the UK government, university courses will be solely assessed on the rate at which a student proceeds through their course of study and then gains what is defined as graduate-level employment. Once implemented, the metric is envisaged to be applied equally to all institutions across the UK irrespective of the social origins of their students, the reasons why they undertake the degree, the way it is studied or even the discipline in which it is studied. Other aspects that are beyond consideration in the metric are the different patterns of engagement that any given individual will decide to take when they are at university and the subsequent influence that this will have on the two parameters that are being measured.

The challenge of understanding the qualitative differences between organisations confirms Hotelling's model of spatial differentiation (Hotelling 1927). In this model, Hotelling sets out to explain consumer choice and offers an effective explanation why businesses of the same type often cluster together in close physical proximity. With minimal differentiation between each business or its offering, it makes economic sense to be located close to a direct competitor in order to attract and draw away the limited pool of total customers from the competing business. The model explains the neighbouring location of ice cream stalls on a beach in the same way as all the guitar shops in a large city are found within a short walk of each other.

Without some recognition within the organisation of its own differences and its capability to express these differences to itself, the likelihood that a visual language or any communication will be able to convey this understanding is slim. Lack of attention to the qualitative elements of an organisation's offering plays into the challenge that an organisation faces when it attempts to report its own activities. The rise of corporate dashboards represents a particular moment in the development of visual management that references the challenge of trying to offer a visual language without recognising that it has an integral relationship with the organisational culture as well as its position in that organisation as one of its tools. Although thinking has been invested in theorising the creation of good and meaningful dashboards (Skorka 2017) the tendency is towards a productised approach that an organisation acquires a dashboard in the same way as any other software – and often from the same vendor – without customisation or naturalisation into that organisation other than the replacement of a logo and adding some corporate colour. With the coarse productisation of dashboard systems, the range of options that a smaller business has to select from is limited still further.

Corporate dashboards take the data that is stored within organisational information systems to represent aspects of that collection. Corporate dashboards provide real-time and immediate representation of the current existing data set held by the organisation. Most dashboards enable some form of querying to drill down and extract specific summaries of parts of this overall dataset. But in many respects, the challenge for these queries is to know what questions to ask – to reveal the unknown unknowns. The value of a massive dataset is in the capacity to discover correlations, overlaps and intersections of attributes and parameters. But to navigate these virtual and dynamic Venn diagrams requires a depth of pre-existing understanding of the data that may not be visible from the view of the corporate dashboard. It can seem like a case of needing to know the answer before the question is asked. It is a case of knowing that the dataset being queried has the relevant data to create the desirable intersections of attributes and that the data required is not held in a still separate, unconnected information system. The 'myth' of dashboards is that the capacity to produce visible end results sits on top of a complete and coherent data representation of the entire organisation. The reality is a disaggregated understanding of the organisation solely represented through the available data that is compatible with the dashboard. Having only a partial view of the entire situation is one of the many organisational maturity issues related to visual management.

Most organisations have either no formal information system or, alternatively, more than one information system. It is a rare thing to find an organisation of any size or scale with exactly one information system. The many organisations with more than one information system often do not possess the capacity to make each 'talk' to one another. More important are the internal information systems that are not formally recognised by the organisation. These informal information systems exist as part of the organisation's culture rather than being part of its IT asset register (Stamper 1993). These systems exist (and persist) through word-of-mouth and through a hidden layer of consumer technology usage (Barmeyer et al. 2019). These are systems that technicians never see, and knowledge management consultants will politely sweep under the carpet. It is in the informal systems where the embedded power of workers exists. Managers rarely encounter them directly, but regularly feel their impact. The systems are only revealed in a positive context at moments of alignment and coherence between workers, management and vision. The challenge is vast and the management maturity required to bring about this type of alignment is significant.

The increasing use of Application Programmers Interface (APIs) is an important step forward for the integration of multiple formal information systems wherever they may exist. Taking this further, it is unlikely that the information systems reporting to dashboards currently take input from the hardware (in the widest sense discussed earlier), processes, communications and people of the organisation in any integrated way. However, with this observation is introduced the world of covert employee tracking that became prevalent during the COVID-19 pandemic (Aloisi and De Stefano 2022), when many white-collar middle-class workers were in a seemingly endless state of working from home. The response of some organisations was to move to a default assumption that the home-based workers were being unproductive and required continuous monitoring during working hours (or even beyond). The increasing digitalisation of the built environment creates smart buildings (and smart homes) that can be monitored continuously and reported back through a dashboard. Collecting relevant data from across the entire organisation – as an information system – is more of a challenge than 'simply' extracting data from well-formed, well-maintained and well-defined datasets used by most existing corporate dashboards.

5   New views on the organisation

Finding patterns in messy data
through the wisdom of the crowd

Visual management is far more than using images instead of text-based documents to report the current situation. At the core of its theorisation is the development of a shared organisational language that embeds patterns of success. The endpoint to this thinking is that visual management is about facilitating the creation and use of a pattern language. Patterns are sense-making recipes that embed learned practices that are known to produce intended positive outcomes (Samson and Challis 2002). Using pattern thinking in organisational management echoes the way that programmers developed a pattern language to present solutions to the most common coding problems in consistent ways that are known to be robust in any programming language (Gamma et al. 1994). Pattern languages originated in architecture with a comprehensive version published for this discipline in 1977 (Alexander et al. 1977). Alexander et al.'s architectural language is even more instructive as an approach than that of the one offered for programming. The patterns that are described systematically work through problems that exist

DOI: 10.4324/9781003304166-5

Table 5.1 A sample of Alexander et al.'s (1977) architectural patterns, including their numbering within the overall list of 253 patterns

1	Independent Regions
5	Lace of Country Streets
19	Web of Shopping
40	Old People Everywhere
56	Bike Paths and Racks
85	Shopfront Schools
124	Activity Pockets
194	Interior Windows
224	Low Doorways
253	Things from Your Life

at a global scale down to the most specific elements, such as giving attention to the details of a window's finish and shape (Table 5.1). Presenting an order for the patterns is done with purpose and emphasises the link between the widest, most encompassing pattern (no. 1) down to the most personal (no. 253). The description of each architectural pattern goes further by showing which other patterns work well together, as well as those that do not. The patterns are presented as short descriptions and many have accompanying explanatory diagrams.

Personal association and lived experience lead thinking down a certain path. Pattern languages – they could be called pattern systems – are instructive for design thinking and sensemaking in the context in which they are being applied. A pattern represents key blocks of understanding within the context of a specific discipline, sector or organisation. They are the consolidation of significant experience and knowledge into a single useful 'boxed-up' solution. Using a pattern successfully is still a skilled task that requires an understanding of context, a stability of surrounding circumstances and a flexibility of thought to make the application of the pattern work in practice. Combined with the embedded knowledge in a pattern is a yearning to not do unnecessary work or 'reinvent the wheel' – a series of observations that reintroduce the FUSY acronym. The original thinking for developing architectural design patterns was that they assisted in resolving conflicting forces regularly encountered by architects rather than setting out a design perspective. The use of the right pattern can lead the individual architect more rapidly down the right path towards an elegant solution for a familiar problem without the pattern having to be detailed, specific or prescriptive. The pattern acts as a piece of consolidated knowledge that is a trigger for imagination as much as it is a safety net.

The TRIZ method (Savransky 2000) for product innovation takes a similar pattern-based approach and endeavours to develop solutions out of conflicting forces. Originally created by Altshuller (Gadd 2002), a Soviet era inventor, TRIZ is premised on the straightforward argument that an improvement in one factor invariably requires the diminishment of another factor. For example, increasing the speed of an object might require a reduction in weight. Identifying the two sides of these contradictions from a list of 39 generic features is the starting point for generating a solution. The list of features is simultaneously the source of the increasing and the decreasing values (Table 5.2). Once the contradiction has been established, the TRIZ method then offers a suggested set of pattern solutions that can be explored to address this combination. A quick scan of the list (Table 5.2) reveals a range of features that have been actively worked upon by, for example, mobile phone manufacturers in the last 20 years. Many of the solutions applied to mobile phone design can be readily identified in the TRIZ list of solutions (Table 5.3). There is evidence of the application of the proposed

Table 5.2 The 39 founding principles of TRIZ for identifying contradictions

1 Weight of moving object	2 Weight of stationary object	3 Length of moving object	4 Length of stationary object
5 Area of moving object	6 Area of stationary object	7 Volume of moving object	8 Volume of stationary object
9 Speed	10 Force	11 Stress or pressure	12 Shape
13 Stability of the object's composition	14 Strength	15 Duration of action by a moving	16 Duration of action by a stationary object
17 Temperature	18 Illumination intensity	19 Use of energy by moving object	20 Use of energy by stationary object
21 Power	22 Loss of Energy	23 Loss of substance	24 Loss of Information
25 Loss of Time	26 Quantity of substance/the matter	27 Reliability	28 Measurement accuracy
29 Manufacturing precision	30 External harm affects the object	31 Object generated harmful factors	32 Ease of manufacture
33 Ease of operation	34 Ease of repair	35 Adaptability or versatility	36 Device complexity
37 Difficulty of detecting and measuring	38 Extent of automation	39 Productivity	

Table 5.3 The original 40 TRIZ solutions

1. Segmentation	2. Extraction (Extracting, Retrieving, Removing)	3. Local Quality	4. Asymmetry
5. Consolidation	6. Universality	7. Nesting	8. Counterweight
9. Prior Counteraction	10. Prior Action	11. Cushion in Advance	12. Equipotentiality
13. Do It in Reverse	14. Spheroidality	15. Dynamicity	16. Partial or Excessive Action
17. Transition into a New Dimension	18. Mechanical Vibration	19. Periodic Action	20. Continuity of Useful Action
21. Rushing through	22. Convert Harm into Benefit	23. Feedback	24. Mediator
25. Self-service	26. Copying	27. Dispose	28. Replacement of Mechanical System
29. Pneumatic or Hydraulic Constructions	30. Flexible Membranes or Thin Films	31. Porous Material	32. Changing the Colour
33. Homogeneity	34. Rejecting and Regenerating Parts	35. Transformation of Properties	36. Phase Transition
37. Thermal Expansion	38. Accelerated Oxidation	39. Inert Environment	40. Composite Materials

solutions in common household items, ranging from the significant development of consumer electric vehicles to the continual reinvention of kitchen gadgets. For any identified contradiction combination, TRIZ offers a sub-set of potential solutions drawn from a total set of forty. In its original form, some contradictions offered no potential solutions or only a single option. Subsequent work has focused on resolving these gaps (Apte and Mann 2002) as well as extending the system with new features and solutions (Ilevbare et al. 2013). The focus of TRIZ was originally used for technical physical products but has since been used in other contexts too, including management change. One of the most extraordinary achievements of TRIZ is that it was developed from the examination of thousands of patent applications with the 39 features and 40 potential solutions extracted manually from this data. Subsequent work has since attempted to extend these solutions using a more computer-based approach to data (Russo and Duci 2015).

The fully manual approach used to generate the solution patterns in TRIZ offers some hope for smaller organisations that they too might be able to engage in the creation of a pattern language relevant to their local situation.

For better resourced organisations, the idea of being to create a pattern language with a more automated approach through the examination of their own data is equally appealing. Taking this claim even further, mining the existing data of a business to define patterns provides a clear rationale for the use of artificial intelligence in a way that gives useful outcomes for a people-first form of management.

While many patterns and even pattern languages are maintained informally within an organisation, there are other formal systems that exhibit the advantages of this approach. In a more management-oriented context, Group Works (groupworksdeck.org) presents, "A Pattern Language for Bringing Life to Meetings and Other Gatherings' – an issue acknowledged by most managers who have been left feeling that the underlying intention of a meeting was not achieved. Unlike other pattern languages, the Group Works project provides a series of patterns that offer solutions to just one problem – 'how to have better meetings'. There is only one contradiction to deal with in this pattern language. Meetings appear to be the best solution for many communications tasks, but the experienced reality of many meetings never seems to realise this imagined potential.

A further pattern language for management addresses another element of working life that promises much and often under-delivers. The Core Protocols (liveingreatness.com/core-protocols/) for team working present a series of patterns for effective behaviour within a team. The Core Protocols have 11 commitments (to the team) that are supported by 11 protocols (for behaviours) that are supported by five additional protocols. These additions represent short activities or forms that consolidate the overall intention of the Core Protocols. Each protocol is composed of a series of steps and a set of commitments along with some guiding notes. The protocols themselves are often binary contrasts such as 'Pass/Unpass', 'Check In' and Check Out', and 'Intention Check' and 'Protocol Check'. The Core Protocols confirm a theme that can be identified through many of the pattern languages. 'Take this work into your life – the more people there are who believe they can make difference, the sooner we will be living in the world we dream of' (Feuer 2010). The accompanying description of ambition for the Core Protocols ties in with the emancipatory perspectives found in Alexander et al. (1977) and to a lesser degree in Altshuller's (Gadd 2002) purpose for TRIZ. The ambition for the creation of Esperanto was similarly emancipatory in that it sought world peace through better mutual understanding (Forster 1982). Making a clear association between patterns and systems of good practice and much wider aspirations for various types of freedoms does make sense. The efficiencies and benefits provided by using known patterns contribute to immediate worker wellbeing on a small scale. The architect creates liveable places, the programming can be confident that their code will be reliable, and successful meetings are motivating and inspiring. In sum, these small beneficial steps contribute to overall satisfaction, better work/life balance and the 'headspace' to explore new ideas and innovate (whether in home or work life). In this way, pattern languages can be seen as entirely people-oriented in purpose and motivation. The people in a system (or in multiple systems) benefit from having a system that is fully functional as a system. People gain freedom because they do not need to act as a proxy for failing communications, missing data, software that is not fit for the required purpose or incomplete definitions of processes. Patterns identify what needs to be done and how it can be done with maximum impact – an optimal combination of flexibility and stability.

Many informal pattern languages that develop over time in an organisation come and go with individuals, as the learning and knowledge is not captured formally and the language may not even be recognised as such by those people who are using it. On rare occasions, individuals in a business may refer to 'The [Organisation] Way', a label for a specific set of learning that is considered distinctive and beneficial. This is a deep manifestation of organisational culture that can be incredibly fragile when it remains undocumented and is reliant on individuals transmitting the learning to colleagues. The University of Manchester's Alliance Business School claims 'The Manchester Method' as 'a highly practical, learning by doing approach to management education, undertaken in a democratic, non-departmental organisation which was only loosely coordinated from the top [which] symbolizes the continuous process of innovation which has typified the approach to course design at Manchester Business School' (Berry 2007). As his 'home' institution, the influence of Stafford Beer, his various thought experiments and projects such as the previously mentioned Cyber-Syn in Chile (Espejo 2014) can be identified in these sentiments. The phrase 'loosely coordinated' particularly resonates closely with this earlier work.

The intersection of culture, systems and organisations alongside the influence of Stafford Beer affirms the concept of the Viable System Model (Beer 1988). The Viable System Model considers the attributes of an organisation that sustains it and ensures it continuity. A viable system is autopoietic – or self-organising, adaptable or flexible, has homeostasis – has stability, is heterogenous in that it is composed of multiple sub-systems and functions and can take a multitude of forms. The Viable System Model (VSM) is composed of five sub-systems, four principles of organisation, three axioms of management and the sub-systems are linked through algedonic signals (Figure 5.1). The final challenging aspect of the model is that it is nested. Viable systems are themselves composed of viable systems (which, coincidentally, is one of the solutions offered by TRIZ – number 7). The VSM makes connections between the operations, management and strategy of

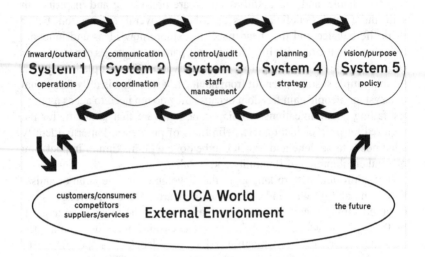

Figure 5.1 The Viable System Model – simplified structure without algedonic signals (Source: after Beer 1988)

the organisation, as well as consciously connecting the organisation with its place and relationship with its environment. Beer's thinking consciously draws on the biological analogy of the brain to describe the VSM. As a result, the model is not hierarchical, as each sub-system needs the other sub-systems to function. There is a balance of autonomy and interdependence between the sub-systems. The algedonic (pleasure/pain) signals of the VSM are a significant acknowledgement within the system that once again recognises the continuous presence of contradictions within a system and the need to resolve these within the system to achieve stability. A description of the attributes of the VSM suggests that Beer was endeavouring to present a type of pattern language for organisations that was founded upon a neurological and cybernetic perspective. There are many commonalities that can be identified in each work despite the fact that, in the case of Beer (1988) and Alexander et al. (1977), they were developed in isolation from one another. However, Gamma et al.'s work (1994) was directly inspired by Alexander et al. (1977) and the influence of Beer on the development of information systems as a discipline which itself has close connections with programming and computer science is potentially an indirect and unrecognised synthesis of these initially separate lines of thinking.

Beer's deep theorisation of the organisation makes it possible to position other thinking and literature regarding organisations as being one or more patterns that can be positioned within his wider system (Beer 1983). Existing literature within management studies could, in extending this line of thinking, be regarded as tacit proposals for patterns within the wider framework of the viable system outlined by Beer. It could further be proposed that the most seminal of management papers represent the leading candidates for inclusion in a general-purpose management pattern language – with their citation counts equating to a form of 'up vote' for each proposal. Taking this observation even further, many of these seminal papers offer a central visual artefact that effectively represents the pattern itself. The Five Forces diagram offered by Porter (1979) is one clear example that helps to feed this speculation. As an example of other pattern contributions, the management novel by Goldratt (1984), The Goal, is simultaneously an exploration in alternative ways of presenting management thought and an example of a prototype for the management pattern language. At the core of the work is the Theory of Constraints. A simplified version of this argument is that as an organisation the route to improvement is to identify the greatest constraint within the organisation and focus all efforts on resolving and improving this weakness until it is an exemplar in the sector. One of its most recent editions (Goldratt et al. 2017) is now presented as a graphic novel (a form of visualisation that follows on from Malcolm MacDonald and Morris's (2000) *Marketing Plan,* which is presented as a pictorial guide for managers).

The similarities in this work to Beer's algedonic signals and Altshuller's contradiction matrix are direct. Goldratt is proposing a solution for balancing out contradictions within the organisation. The pattern is generalisable, with its core purpose being improvement. Some managers and theorists disagree with Goldratt's approach – another feature of patterns is that not all work in all situations. Other methods, including especially marginal gain (Ahmed et al. 1999) or incremental improvement, are a favoured alternative with analogies drawn from the approach and success of the British Cycling Team (Hall et al. 2012). The elegance of a pattern language – and any language – is the ability to express multiple alternative points of view without breaking the system. Marginal gain is a management pattern for improvement that is different from Goldratt's, but both could be used in an organisation. More formal pattern languages, including Alexander et al. (1977) explicitly identifies combinations of patterns that are incompatible as well as suggesting those that work well together.

In any organisational context, taking learning from the messy data of a business is itself challenging. Identifying patterns amongst this learning can be even more challenging. In contrast to generalised pattern language generation, the learned patterns of success within a business will have specific organisational context – encapsulating the variations in purpose, mission and vision that exist between every organisation. There is the additional parameter of the difference created by each organisational culture. The potential to use the larger generalised patterns of management is possible because of the wisdom of the wider crowd at large. Within the context of organisational culture, the crowd who can bring a specific depth of knowledge about the organisation is more restricted. The key parameters of culture, purpose, vision and mission applied to the generation of a pattern language further emphasise the importance of the longer-term project of an organisational language that captures the knowledge and learning of its own people over time. Maintaining the connection between organisational vision and all its people must take advantage of the stored wisdom of that culture, in the sense that there is a collective awareness of the patterns of success within all aspects of the organisation's activities. With this realisation comes the further conclusion that recognising, learning and extracting the patterns of success that exist amongst the current culture is best achieved through easily created and communicated visual techniques.

The development of an organisational language does not commence with a blank sheet. It is a process of synthesis in the Hegelian dialectic sense (Figure 5.2). Existing management theory provides the theses, and the organisational culture provides multiple antitheses – the contradictions in practice. The process of resolution – the construction of synthesis – requires the resolution of the specific organisational challenges in relation to an individual management theory – or pattern of success. Viewed in this way, the creation of an organisational language recognises the role and impact of

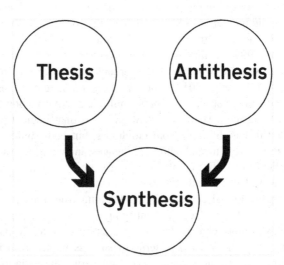

Figure 5.2 Hegelian dialect as a form of organisational pattern language generation

change while being part of it. Considering the number of organisations that exist at any given moment, their individual differences and specific context, the chance that any management theory will relate to that specific combination of circumstances might be seen as negligible. The situation means that the generalised situation being imagined or described by an academic paper has contradictions when it is applied to any individual organisation. As the author of a paper that specifically names a commercial organisation in its title (Heinze et al. 2018) it is clear that the process of describing a model in increasingly general terms will move it away from the specific experience found inside the company that was observed. Synthesising local culture with generalised patterns of action is one opportunity for the many theories of business that remain generally unrealised in terms of creating research impact. This synthesis risks moving an organisation towards generalisation and obscurity. By simply seeing an academic theory as a template that is 'filled in' instead of being used as an insightful pattern to synthesise around local conditions then risks organisational distinctiveness being pushed aside.

As a further step in the development of organisational patterns and a system of patterns, there is the metaprocess described by a pattern language for pattern languages (Iba and Isaku 2016). There are several formal and informal proposals for pattern language creation. However, the Iba Lab version is extensive and founded upon their own prior development of other pattern languages for organisation around areas such as presentation and project design as well as languages for wellbeing, including living with dementia (Iba and Isaku 2016). The Iba Lab meta-pattern language contains 364 patterns and is pyramidal in its design to aid comprehension with three separate branches of pattern discovery, writing and symbolising. These three branches then fork off into three separate branches and onwards over five levels of hierarchy. Importantly, for the discussion in this book, a key component of the symbolising part of language creation is an entire hierarchy created for 'Image Drawing', which contains patterns such as 'Stand in the Scene', 'Line of Expression', 'Image Depth' and 'Natural Expressions'. Within their description of the language, pencil sketch images are used to complement the pattern descriptions down to its fourth level of hierarchy.

Other systems for improving strategy and generating change have been regularly productised. These examples are often presented as card decks. It is a trend that follows on from an early project by Brian Eno and Peter Schmidt when they created 'Oblique Strategies' to encourage greater creativity (www.enoshop.co.uk/product/oblique-strategies.html). The deck of cards could be considered as prototype patterns for action with some of the statements being open ended or provocative rather than outlining a generalised solution (stoney.sb.org/eno/oblique.html), for example, 'Are there sections? Consider transitions', 'Tidy Up' and 'Towards the Insignificant'.

But considering the original design statement for Oblique Strategies, these could all be arguably regarded as fully formed patterns that would prompt creativity and, hence, do succeed in their intended purpose.

As a more recent example, the Terra Prime card deck describes itself on Kickstarter as a conversation deck and educational tool (www.kickstarter.com/projects/1211246733/terra-prime-a-conversation-deck-and-educational-tool). The format takes a familiar form that emphasises the role of the visual in initiating complex conversations. The deck takes advantage of its card format to offer a highly visual face accompanied by a provocative phrase that is supported on the reverse by a prompt, questions, keywords and an exercise. It is a format that closely mirrors the structure used by many of the pattern languages already discussed here.

The many examples of generalised systems designed to bring about improvement as well as removing the need for people to personally redis-cover well-trodden and necessary practices within specific industries (e.g. patternlanguageforgamedesign.com) provides strong indication that the wisdom of the crowd is readily available. What is generally missing is the more difficult guidance on how to take this thesis – the knowledge – and undertake the synthesis with the antithesis of the organisation itself. It is a challenging process, as the dialectic brings two-way change to the the-sis and antithesis in the process of reaching synthesis. For managers, the change that is being sought in the organisational situation may be the culture itself. But culture is resilient and, from a dialectic perspective, influences the intended change itself. Information Systems literature acknowledges the two-way influence by describing the rise of 'workarounds' that occurs dur-ing and after an unsuccessful system implementation (Spierings et al. 2017). With the designation as 'unsuccessful' being the managerial (and generally negative) viewpoint of the type of synthesis that has occurred.

As with all activities in an organisation, change resolves back to being fundamentally about people. Digital transformation represents the current label for organisational change practice, but when change is enacted under this banner that exclusively focuses on software, data, processes or com-munications without engaging people, it invariably underdelivers or simply fails (Kozak-Holland and Procter 2020). Iba Lab's (Iba and Isaku 2016) language recognises the human factors in its mining patterns, with a specific section described as experience mining. In terms of producing synthesis, the experience mining pattern sets out to understand how the change envisaged by the introduction of external ideas will be internalised and the degree to which it will be accepted. Taking this line of thought comes back to the pri-mary rationale of organisations (Chapter 1), that is, to manage its relation-ship to the threat of the external VUCA world.

Engaging a wider variety of people in the initial practices of synthesis encourages internal transparency and openness to address real and imagined contradictions from the start. Legacy manifests in so many ways within an organisation – through software, processes and communication – all of these are proxies for earlier forms of culture and former people associated with the organisation carried through into the present. Legacy combined with the resistance of current people expressed through the culture of an organisation are the antithesis to change. An observation that closely mirrors the observation that 'culture eats strategy' (Engel 2018), although this statement overly disentangles strategy from organisational culture – of which it is a part rather than being a counterforce. Similarly, definitions such as 'Cultural change is the process in which an organization encourages employees to adopt behaviours and mindsets that are consistent with the organization's values and goals' (Gartner n.d.) adopt a clearly managerialist view of the organisation by separating the organisation from the employees and setting out a tension between the culture of employees and the organisation's values. The influence of overly structured theorisations of culture or models intended to enable comparisons of difference, such as Hofstede (2011) and Murdock (1967), influence these types of perspectives as they seemingly create a sense that culture has a quality of measurability and then reveal a clear dialectic that can be resolved (in terms of management action). A more culturalist approach regards continuous change as an inherent aspect of any culture and that the collection of commonly shared beliefs and values of a group of people defines a culture (Katzenbach et al. 2012). Sub-cultures are themselves defined by a sub-set of beliefs and values that they hold that contradict that of a dominant mainstream. Viewed in these terms within the context of organisations serves to remove the overtly hierarchical implications in the Gartner definition to potentially position 'managers' and 'employees' as members of different (organisational) sub-cultures – while highlighting the role of the interdependent systems found in Beer's Viable System Model. Conflict occurs when one sub-culture presumes to 'own' the organisation rather than more modestly being its current custodians.

How change is observed to occur within cultural groups – beyond those of the organisation – can then be instructive to understanding how patterns can be synthesised into the organisation. Many examples of change can be reduced to a few appeals to the tendencies of human nature. Actions are made easier, threats are reduced, and opportunities for leisure over work are increased, provided that recognised and existing lifeways are maintained or improved. New inventions and processes are more likely to find favour with individuals if these conditions are met. Culture is a mediating influence. In a pseudo-statistical sense, culture could even be described as the median of all the experiences of the individuals in a cultural group combined. Individuals will accept and undertake change to differing degrees based on the extent of the change. Some will change for a marginal benefit while others will resist until no viable alternative remains – this is a restating of the diffusion of innovation model (MacVaugh and Schiavone 2010) now applied to organisational change (Figure 5.3).

These threads all link back to the benefits of visual management and a system-oriented perspective on the organisation (Figure 5.4).

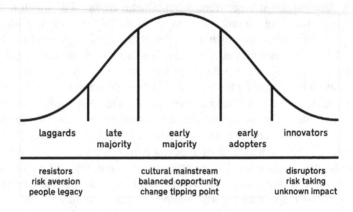

Figure 5.3 A restatement of the diffusion of innovation model in relation to cultural change

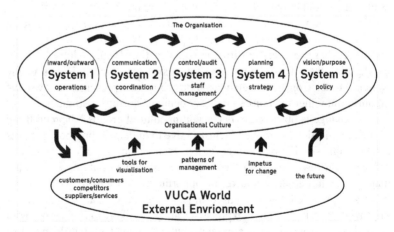

Figure 5.4 Organisations, patterns, culture and change

(Source: after Beer 1988)

6 Building blocks for practical visual management

Tools and a typology of visualisation techniques

The smallest elements for visual management can be identified in the existing works of academic, grey literature and organisational documentation. These are the sources of potential management patterns that have been described previously (Chapter 5). Many of these works utilise individual visual artefacts to communicate the essence of their meaning. What can be seen from this previous literature is a typology of the symbols and techniques of visualisation that can be used consistently and with purpose in organisational communication for the purpose of bringing beneficial change. The literature includes forms such as the 2 × 2 grid used as the 'Boston Consulting Group Matrix' – ⊞, the 'Bar Graph' – 📊, and the circular feedback loop – ↺ – preferred by the Gibbs's (1988) reflective cycle and Goldratt's (1984) Theory of Constraints (Figure 6.2). Systematic analysis of visual symbols has previously been taken further with the periodic table of visualisation developed by Visual Literacy (visual-literacy.org) and subsequently used in other papers and writings (e.g. Oliveira et al. 2017) (Table 6.1). Other categorisations of visualisation techniques also offer different forms of clustering (Vital 2018). There is no consistent language for visualisation. The typology of the visual forms documents the readily available syntax that can provide the techniques for an organisation's visual language. Creating symbols and combining them to produce more specific meanings

DOI: 10.4324/9781003304166-6

is the syntax of the language. The semantics, however, sit primarily with the people – who speak it – and organisational culture – that perpetuates it.

Taking inspiration from the advice of Iba Labs (Iba and Isaku 2016) to pattern mine for patterns combined with the existing typology of visualisation provides guidance for sourcing the key symbols for visual management. Unicode has already been cited as well as being directly used in this and the previous chapters, as a system for representing symbols of any language. It is another influence showing what is easily possible for any organisation that enables it to visually represent its activities. The capability of Unicode to modify other symbols – primarily intended to add diacritical marks – can then be taken to an extreme through, for example, Zalgo, which is intended for creative purposes by overloading the originally intended use by combining many sub- and super-scripts (Figure 6.1). The example of Zalgo and other 'art with words' such as Matrix indicate that the flexibility of expression that is possible with conventional textual digital communications approaches that of pen and paper but in a way that is exponentially easier to share with a wider audience. However, the purpose of this chapter is not to invent symbols for management that are more difficult to use than existing textual description but to define what existing symbols and visualisation techniques can already be applied to management.

As the previous chapter highlighted, academic and consultant perspectives on management practices tend to address the planning and strategic aspects of the viable system in its semantics. These are the aspects of an organisation's activities that do tend to be more qualitative until they are turned into SMART objectives that necessarily place a quantitative value

Figure 6.1 An example of Zalgo

(Source: created using piliapp.com/cool-text/zalgo-text/)

of measurement against each parameter that is regarded as important. In contrast, the visualisations that are produced in the reporting back of activities tend to be operational and embedded in the software tools used for the analysis (Chapter 4). While the language (or the dialect) of reporting is an integral part of the organisation, as it is a direct result of its planning and actions, the techniques and symbols that are used come from somewhere external to the organisation. The situation is a result of less critical attention being given to the artefacts created because they are 'automatically' generated by Excel, PowerBI, SPSS or other more customised software. The automatic acceptance of the output from a specific piece of software happens regularly in academic writing.

As a case that makes this point, a personal example is appropriate. In authoring a chapter that was based on the textual analysis of a corpus that had been created over a 50-year period, I and a colleague made use of Sinclair and Rockwell's Voyant Tools (voyant-tools.org). We were particularly keen to identify the changing emphasis of specific phrases used during the period of the corpus and used one of the Voyant Tools to extract the information. The paper discussed the implications of what was revealed and connected these findings with wider trends within the discipline. Initial feedback from the peer reviewers was positive regarding the direction of the chapter and the figures that were included we believed had concisely summarised the trends that we were reporting. At the final round of review, a senior editor presented some very strong objections about the paper. The concern was not about the key argument or case that the chapter was presenting but the way that the figures were being presented visually. As authors, we had taken the output of Voyant Tools – a line graph – and transposed these artefacts directly into the chapter with suitable acknowledgements. The editor's concern rightly recognised that the values were discrete and that a line graph implied continuity between each of the reported values. After some hurried recalculation and redrawing of the figures into more suitable bar graphs, an improved manuscript was submitted. As authors of the chapter, we had directly taken the output and uncritically presented these representations and as a result privileged the software (as excellent as it is) and gave up some of our own agency in the authoring process.

A further example seen through my own 'manager' perspective is the process of producing strategic plans and their translation into actions. Going through the process of creating strategies for varying purposes, it becomes evident very rapidly that the narrative being created is quickly overlooked for the action plan that is derived from the lengthier statements. The actions have defined and measurable outcomes. As a result, the creation of the strategy itself is at risk of being reduced to a personal journaling activity that is needed to generate the actions. But, on occasion, the organisational feedback will be that the outcomes that measure the success of the individual action cannot be used because existing systems cannot easily report on the proposed measures. The path of least resistance – and not the best option – is to change the outcomes to match an available 'next best' measure. The more appropriate, but more complex, course of action would be to explore how the desired measures could be reported as well as being in a form that can be readily understood by the audience, who eventually will make further decisions based on these documented outcomes.

These vignettes provide a personal emphasis on the way the intentions of planning and the realities of reporting can become separated and diminish the value of different visualisations in their intended context. The Visual Literacy periodic table provides three dimensions in the classification of the visualisations that it catalogues, and this offers some guidance as to the selection of the optimal visualisation for any given requirement. Specific visualisations are labelled as being exclusively data, information, concept, strategy, metaphor or compound. However, the classification system somewhat bends this rule of exclusivity (at a visual level) by using the same form in different categories with new labels. Thus, while 'Cartesian Coordinates' are presented as a data visualisation technique, the 'Magic Quadrant', 'BCG Matrix' and 'Stakeholder Rating Map' (Figure 6.2) are shown as being for strategy visualisation despite following the same familiar 2 × 2 grid. These types of visual overlaps are potential pointers for reconciling and linking the realms of an organisation's reporting with that of its planning. Each visualisation technique identified by Visual Literacy is assigned with additional parameters and marked as being process or structure as well as convergent or divergent thinking. Using these classifications in combination holds the potential to identify a preferred technique for any specific purpose. The periodic table (itself a visualisation technique not acknowledged by Visual Literacy) frames a way to find the most suitable type of visualisation based on its intended purpose rather than based on what is available in a piece of software or is known to individuals within an organisation. The multidimensional classification highlights that while some visualisation techniques may be different to look at, the way in which they are used is similar. For example, and not surprisingly, all the data visualisation techniques are classified as representing both structure and convergent thinking. Information visualisation techniques do have more variations but only 'semantic network' and 'clustering' offer divergent thinking perspectives.

Taking this classification approach further offers a way of refining the request for a visualisation without necessarily having to already know what the outcome will look like. A system specifically intended for management should be able to consider additional definitional classes and provide further refinement to the scheme. These classes can include planning or reporting;

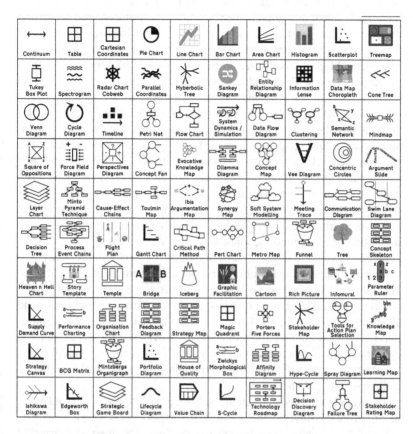

Figure 6.2 A summary of visualisation techniques identified by the periodic table of Visual Literacy

internal, external or a combination to identify the likely intended audience; qualitative or quantitative; as well as tactical or strategic purpose. Taking the combination of a systems-oriented and artefact approach, it is possible to define whether the visualisation is intended for immediate communication or is to be more permanent as a documented process or by being embedded into hardware such as signage. Additional considerations of this type may influence the choice of visualisation. For example, the intention to have greater permanence because it will influence the organisational culture into the future will require greater adherence to a coherent visual language for the organisation. This is particularly true of compound visualisation techniques in the Visual Literacy catalogue: the 'Cartoon', 'Rich Picture', 'Knowledge

Map', 'Learning Map' and 'Infomural' (Figure 6.2). The extent to which these more intentionally permanent artefacts can influence the future and the organisation itself can clearly be seen in one visualisation technique defined for use as a metaphorical technique, the 'Metro Map' (Figure 6.2). The Metro Map is a well used technique, but it is heavily derived from the initial work of Beck and his method of displaying the Underground routes across London (Garland 1994). The form is not a literal geographic presentation which explains its classification as a technique for metaphors. Tourists mistakenly attempt to navigate London on foot using the current map (Vertesi 2008) and Transport for London, which now runs the whole transport network, changed the symbol for its bus service to match that of the Underground (London Transport Museum n.d.). Books have been dedicated to the map and what it endeavoured to do (Garland 1994; Roberts 2005) and there is constant debate about the best and worst versions of the map over its history (Roberts 2005). The map's approach has been repeated in multiple ways around the globe with varying degrees of success. Most perpetuate some of the key features introduced by Beck, such as black hollow circles for junctions, multiple distinct colours to distinguish different lines, and careful placement of text to keep everything horizontal (and readable) (Roberts 2005). Beck's map now represents Transport for London and all London public transport and defines the visual language of the organisation for the commuting public. Internally, the evidence for this language is only slightly hinted at within Transport for London's strategy and planning documents (content.tfl.gov.uk/bus-action-plan.pdf; content.tfl.gov.uk/mts-walking-action-plan.pdf).

The ways in which visualisation can bring greater transparency and openness to an organisation (Kennedy et al. 2016) shapes other criteria for interpreting available visualisation approaches as artefacts. The question of whether the visualisation is offered for further participatory inscription by its intended audience or is presented as already complete will shape selection preferences. The Business Model Canvas (Osterwalder and Pigneur 2013) and how it is used within an organisation expresses the challenge within this delineation. The Business Model Canvas is not directly represented in the Visual Literacy scheme (Table 6.1), but its base influences can be readily recognised. The Canvas is strategic, represents a convergence of thinking and is structural. With this interpretation, the relationship to the 'BCG Matrix', 'Strategy Map' and 'Porter's Five Forces' are all evident (Figure 6.2). But presented as a completed work, the Business Model Canvas could be interpreted as a 'Cartoon' or 'Graphic Facilitation' (Figure 6.2). While this may sometimes be the intention when it is shown to an external audience, much of the value in using the Business Model Canvas is the way it can capture a range of internal perspectives from across an organisation (Griffiths and Fletcher 2020).

Table 6.1 Classification of Visualisation Techniques clustered by tentative classifications

Form	Type	Process / Structure	Divergent / Convergent	Planning / Reporting	Permanent/Temporary	Internal/External	Qualitative/ Quantitative	Strategic/Tactical	Editing/Disseminating	Editable/Not Editable (Word or Excel
Continuum	Data	S	C	P	T	I	QL	S	E	E
Table	Data	S	C	P/R	T	I/E	QL/QN	S/T	E	E
Cartesian Coordinates	Data	S	C	R	T	I/E	QN	S/T	D	N
Pie Chart	Data	S	C	R	T	I/E	QN	S/T	D	N
Line Chart	Data	S	C	R	T	I/E	QN	S/T	D	N
Bar Chart	Data	S	C	R	T	I/E	QN	S/T	D	N
Area Chart	Data	S	C	R	T	I/E	QN	S/T	D	N
Histogram	Data	S	C	R	T	I/E	QN	S/T	D	N
Scatterplot	Data	S	C	R	T	I	QN	T	D	N
Tukey Box Plot	Data	S	C	R	T	I/E	QN	T	D	N
Spectrogram	Data	S	C	R	T	I	QN	T	D	N
Radar Chart/Cobweb	Information	S	C	R	T	I/E	QN	S/T	D	N
Parallel Coordinates	Information	S	C	R	T	I/E	QN	S/T	D	N
Hyperbolic Tree	Information	S	C	R	P	I/E	QL	S	D	N

(*Continued*)

Table 6.1 (Continued)

Form	Type	Process / Structure	Divergent / Convergent	Planning / Reporting	Permanent/Temporary	Internal/External	Qualitative/ Quantitative	Strategic/Tactical	Editing/Disseminating	Editable/Not Editable (Word or Excel
Sankey Diagram	Information	S	C	R	T	I	QN	T	D	N
Information Lens	Information	S	C	R	T	I	QN	S	D	N
Entity Relationship Diagram	Information	S	C	P/R	P	i/E	QL	S	D/E	N
Data Map (or Choropleth)	Information	S	C	P/R	P	I/E	QN	S	D	N
Treemap	Information	S	C	R	T	I	QN	S	D	N
Cone Tree	Information	S	C	R	T/P	I/E	QL	S	D	N
Venn Diagram	Information	S	C	P/R	T/P	I	QL	S/T	E	E
Cycle Diagram	Information	P	C	P	P	I/E	QL	S	D	N
Timeline	Information	P	C	P	P	I/E	QL	S	D	N
Petri Net	Information	P	C	P	T	I	QL	T	D	N
Flow Chart	Information	P	C	P	P	I	QL	T	D	N
System Dynamics/Simulation	Information	P	C	P	P	I	QL	T	D	N
Data Flow Diagram	Information	P	C	P	P	I	QL	T	D	N
Clustering	Information	S	D	P/R	P	I/E	QL	S	D	N
Semantic Network	Information	S	D	R	T	I	QL	T	D	N

Mindmap	Concept	S	D	P	T/P	I	QL	S	D	N
Square of Oppositions	Concept	S	D	P/R	T/P	I	QL	S	D	E
Force Field Diagram	Concept	S	D	P/R	T/P	I	QL	S	D	E
Perspectives Diagram	Concept	S	D	P	T	I	QL	S	E	E
Concept Fan	Concept	S	D	P/R	T/P	I	QL	S	D	E
Evocative Knowledge Map	Concept	S	D	P/R	T/P	I	QL	S	D	E
Dilemma Diagram	Concept	S	C	P/R	T/P	I	QL	S	D	E
Concept Map	Concept	S	C	P	P	I	QL	S	D	N
Vee Diagram	Concept	S	C	P	P	I	QL	S	D	N
Concentric Circles	Concept	S	C	P	P	I	QL	S	D	E
Argument Slide	Concept	S	C	P	P	I	QL	S	D	N
Layer Chart	Concept	S	C	P/R	P	I/E	QL	S	D	N
Minto Pyramid Technique	Concept	S	C	P	P	I	QL	S	E	E
Cause-Effect Chains	Concept	S	C	P	P	I	QL	S	E	E
Toulmin Map	Concept	S	C	P	T	I	QL	T	D/E	E
Ibis Argumentation Map	Concept	S	C	P/R	T	I	QL	T	D/E	E
Synergy Map	Concept	S	-	P/R	T	I	QL	T	D	N
Concept Skeleton	Concept	S	C	P	T/P	I	QL	S	D	E
Soft System Modelling	Concept	P	C	P	T/P	I	QL	S/T	D	E
Meeting Trace	Concept	P	C	R	T	I/E	QL	T	D	E
Communication Diagram	Concept	P	C	P/R	T	I	QL	T	D	E
Swim Lane Diagram	Concept	P	C	P	T	I	QL	T	D	N

(Continued)

Table 6.1 (Continued)

Form	Type	Process / Structure	Divergent / Convergent	Planning / Reporting	Permanent/Temporary	Internal/External	Qualitative/ Quantitative	Strategic/Tactical	Editing/Disseminating	Editable/Not Editable (Word or Excel
Decision Tree	Concept	P	C	P	T	I	QL	T	D	E
Process Event Chains	Concept	P	C	P	T	I	QL	T	D	N
Flight Plan	Concept	P	C	P	T	I	QL	T	D	E
Gantt Chart	Concept	P	C	P	T	I	QL	T	D	E
Critical Path Method	Concept	P	C	P	T	I	QN/QL	T	D	N
Pert Chart	Concept	P	C	P	T	I	QN/QL	T	D	N
Metro Map	Metaphor	P	C	R	P	E	QL	S	D	N
Funnel	Metaphor	P	C	P/R	P	I/E	QL	S	D	N
Tree	Metaphor	S	C	P	P	I/E	QL	S	D	N
Parameter Ruler	Metaphor	S	D	P	P	I	QL	T	D	N
Heaven 'n Hell Chart	Metaphor	S	D	P	P	I	QL	T	D	E
Story Template	Metaphor	S	D	P	T	I	QL	S	E	E
Temple	Metaphor	P	-	P	T	I	QL	T	D	N
Bridge	Metaphor	P	-	P	T	I	QL	S	D	E
Iceberg	Metaphor	P	-	P	T	I	QL	S	D	

Graphic Facilitation	Compound	S	-	P	P	I	QL	S/T	D	N
Cartoon	Compound	S	-	P/R	P	I/E	QL	S	D	N
Rich Picture	Compound	S	-	P/R	P	I/E	QL	S/T	D	N
Knowledge Map	Compound	S	-	P/R	P	I/E	QL	S/T	D	N
Infomural	Compound	S	-	P/R	P	I/E	QL	S/T	D	N
Learning Map	Compound	P	-	P/R	P	I/E	QL	S/T	D	N
Supply Demand Curve	Strategy	S	C	P	T	I	QN	S/T	D	E
Performance Charting	Strategy	S	C	P/R	T	I	QL	T	D/E	E
Organisation Chart	Strategy	S	C	P/R	P	I/E	QL	S	D/E	E
Feedback Diagram	Strategy	S	C	R	T	I	QL	T	E	E
Strategy Map	Strategy	S	C	P	T	I	QL	S	D/E	E
Magic Quadrant	Strategy	S	C	P/R	T	I	QN/QL	S	D/E	E
Porter's Five Forces	Strategy	S	C	P/R	T	I	QL	S	D	E
Stakeholder Map	Strategy	S	C	P/R	T	I	QL	S	D	E
Tools for Action Plan Selection	Strategy	S	C	P	T	I	QL	S	D	N
Stakeholder Rating Map	Strategy	S	C	P/R	T	I	QN/QL	S	D	N
Strategy Canvas	Strategy	S	C	P/R	T	I	QN/QL	S	D	E
BCG Matrix	Strategy	S	C	P	T	I	QN/QL	S	D	E
Mintzberg's Organigraph	Strategy	S	C	P	P/T	I/E	QL	S	D	N
Portfolio Diagram	Strategy	S	C	P/R	P/T	I/E	QN/QL	S	D	E
House of Quality	Strategy	S	D	P/R	P	I	QL	S	D	N
Zwicky's Morphological Box	Strategy	S	D	P/R	T	I	QL	T	D/E	E

(Continued)

Table 6.1 (Continued)

Form	Type	Process / Structure	Divergent / Convergent	Planning / Reporting	Permanent/Temporary	Internal/External	Qualitative/ Quantitative	Strategic/Tactical	Editing/Disseminating	Editable/Not Editable (Word or Excel)
Affinity Diagram	Strategy	S	D	P/R	T	I	QL	S	D	E
Spray Diagram	Strategy	S	D	P/R	T	I	QL	T	D	E
Failure Tree	Strategy	S	-	R	T	I	QL	T	D	N
Ishikawa Diagram	Strategy	S	-	P/R	T	I/E	QL	S	D	N
Edgeworth Box	Strategy	S	-	P/R	T	I	QN/QL	T	D	E
Strategic Game Board	Strategy	P	C	P	P	I/E	QL	S	D	N
Lifecycle Diagram	Strategy	P	C	P	P	I/E	QN/QL	S	D	N
Value Chain	Strategy	P	D	P/R	T	I	QL	S	D	E
S-Cycle	Strategy	P	D	P/R	T	I	QN/QL	S	D	E
Hype-Cycle	Strategy	P	D	P/R	T	I	QN/QL	S	D	E
Technology Roadmap	Strategy	P	-	P	T	I	QL	S	D	E
Decision Discovery Diagram	Strategy	P	-	P	T	I	QL	T	D	N

(Source: after Visual Literacy incorporating tentative classification of auxiliary parameters – Table 6.2)

Table 6.2 Table of parameters for choosing visualisation techniques

Structure	Process
Convergent thinking	Divergent thinking
Planning	Reporting
Permanent	Temporary
Internal audience	External audience
Qualitative	Quantitative
Strategic	Tactical
Intended for editing	Intend for disseminating
Can be generally edited	Cannot be generally edited

The Business Model Canvas is designed to be used in this collaborative way. The Business Model Canvas highlights an additional classification criterion for management visualisations. Going beyond the *intention* for a visualisation to be inscribed by different people is the *capability* for the visualisation to be easily shared for inscription using tools such as Word or Excel. The advantage of complex images as a single package is that each can be easily shared through social media and other channels (Zer-Aviv 2014), but this benefit runs counter to the capability for further inscription. This nearly explains the problem with information graphics used inside an organisation. The issue of capability, like intent, goes beyond the representation of the visualisation itself and introduces the context of the organisation and of technology. Arguably, all the visualisation techniques in the Visual Literacy table could be inscribed and shared across an organisation. The reality is much more variable. The compound techniques such as 'Learning Map' require access to vector editing software and that the map has been composed and saved in multiple layers. These technical conditions need to be met even before consideration is given to the 'I can't draw' pushback from individuals (Fisher 2021) and a general human tendency not to want to 'deface' an existing image. Similarly, many data and information visualisations imply an authoritative source that cannot simply be changed and in examples such as a 'Tukey Box Plot' (Figure 6.2), there may be limited capacity outside a software package to calculate the needed median and standard deviation values. Consideration of how a specific technique can be authored is a further rationale for the regular appearance of the 2 × 2 form of grid appearing in academic and organisational visualisations. It is a form that can be presented in a Word or Excel document and could even be presented in a simple text document with the careful combination of the -, + and | characters or with the Unicode equivalents of ─, ┼ and │. Because it is primarily composed of boxes, the Business Model Canvas can be recreated in a similar manner in a Word or Excel document to be shared and easily edited by anyone. An observation that might explain its popularity and adoption in such a wide range of organisations.

The separation of how planning is done and the reporting of completed activities is a two-sided challenge for creating a genuinely useful and integrated approach to visual management (Figure 6.2). What is needed is a meaningful loop between planning and reporting that is not only visual in its approach but is part of a consistent common language that enables reporting to be iteratively integrated into further planning and further consolidated as learned patterns of success. A clear separation of organisational functions is an unfamiliar one to most startups and microbusinesses, where close alignment is generally embodied in the small number of people involved. As organisations grow, their complexity increases and the separation of individual functions, activities and reporting from vision becomes more acute. Looking at Beer's (1988) Viable System Model, it is as though the gaps between the five systems increase as the organisation itself grows. To use a visual analogy, internally, among the founders the vision for growth might be described as 🌳 but among new employees this same success might be stated as 🌳 and in reporting to potential investors the materials produced by an external agency is saying that it is 🌴. These statements are similar in intent, but each brings a slightly different nuance to the situation. The challenge for the growing organisation is to recognise its patterns of success in that growth and to express them consistently across the newly enlarged entity. The action required is not to impose the definition of 🌳 but to understand why and how 🌳 and 🌴 have come to exist with meaning and to recognise that the evolving reality requires an agreeable synthesis, with, for example, 🌲. Admittedly, this is an overly figurative way to put the point, but the statement is clear (and fortunately there are four different tree emojis readily available in Unicode).

The underlying challenge that can be seen in the artificial separating out of reporting software is the need to create a critical discourse around software and the artefacts that they produce. The goal is to create an organisational language that is not just a 'dialect' of Excel or similar software without having to directly resort to the core building blocks of visualisation through, for example, the D3 software library (d3js.org). The objective is to achieve a synthesis of external knowledge and the internal culture. Larger organisations may have the computing skills to explore this second option, but it remains an action largely outside the resources of smaller businesses.

The limitations of readily available and popular commercial software restrict what is currently possible from a visual management point of view. It is not a case that existing software is not capable of representing activity in visually engaging ways – in some respects, it can be the opposite issue. Popular productivity software is designed to be used in so many situations without any consideration for the specific organisational context where it is being utilised – it covers all the available possibilities through maximum generalisation. Designing for the most generic use cases is a necessary approach in creating productivity software – from a vendor's perspective – as anything that limits who can use the software would be a restriction on uptake, popularity and sales. The result is too much flexibility and no representation of the organisation and its culture within the software itself. For example, the ability to use stylesheets within Word provides a very low-level example of how an organisation can maintain consistency across all its written communications, but so many people are not trained or aware of how to use stylesheets in a document. In Word, it is easier to write without using stylesheets than it is to create, apply or override a style. Using the easiest *ad hoc* method offers no organisational context or structure, ultimate flexibility and no need for any critical discourse about how the tool is used. However, using Word in the loosest possible way does result in giving up access to some of the features that the software offers. For example, automatically generating a table of contents requires a well-structured document that has been defined using stylesheets. Using the properties of a document enables the definition of keywords and a summary that could be used meaningfully within an organisation and even identify commonalities and overlaps (through metadata such as user-defined keywords) between individual work. Benefiting fully from the software requires a more conscious approach to the use of Word and an organisational infrastructure that sits beyond individual desktops. Instead, the context of Word is really the software company that creates it – and subsequently how the document creation capabilities of Word integrate with the other software and systems that the same vendor produces. Attempting to impose organisational rulesets on these tools creates a fragile operating environment and one that is more fragile than no rulesets at all. It should be acknowledged that while Microsoft's products are the most discussed in relation to this perspective on software, other vendors who focus their products within specific sectors have tackled the problem of productising organisational tools in the same way – that is, to make it as applicable as possible to as many identifiable use cases as possible. CAD, graphic design, bookkeeping and HR recruitment systems can all be evaluated in the same manner to reach the same conclusion. The situation produces something of an inevitable bind for organisations. The yearning for software that enables a consistent organisational language that represents its culture and purpose might be high, but it is something out of reach to the smallest due to the cost of commissioned software. For the largest organisations, more hierarchical management structures and larger IT teams may bring in mechanisms to impose stability and consistency, but this generally can only occur at a superficial and surface level through templates or with additional labour with layers of editorial control and supervision (depending on the nature of the organisation). Still, in all situations, the cost is a factor. Creating robust networked systems for use across multiple sites is even more expensive and for most businesses, creating software for use at this scale and purpose is not within their organisation's core skills.

The reasons for the ensuing free-for-all stems from the long-term success and dominance of the individual products themselves. For example, the core set of Microsoft Office tools have evolved from a period before widespread networked computing existed. It was a time when the idea of sharing documents electronically was relatively limited and the ability to do things such as the simultaneous editing of a document was still effectively over a generation away into the future. Like many software developments, Word has continuously evolved over this time to incorporate more recent innovations and preferences within personal and business computing. There have been some false turns in this history, but overwhelmingly Word (and other software of similar longevity) is the sum total of these combined lessons and additions with a central function that remains largely unchanged from its original inception. The organisational perspective – at the same time as Word and other productivity tools first became available – were to just encourage the use of word processing, spreadsheets or other digital tools without imposing any further restrictions on how they should be used. The enlightened thinking among managers at the time was that just having digital artefacts was better than having paper equivalents. *Ad hoc* ways of working with software are now an ingrained aspect of most organisational cultures.

At the same time, there is a limit to the flexibility offered by tools such as Excel. A direct contradiction to the previous comments regarding Word, anyone can produce visualisations with Excel but only within a narrow subset of the types described by the Visual Literacy periodic table of techniques. Depending on the installed version of Excel, this sub-set is currently around seventeen types that sit within the data and information classification types. Visualisation techniques such as 'Pie Chart', 'Bar Chart', 'Area Chart' and 'Cartesian Coordinates' (Figure 6.2) are the most common forms that are offered (and used). With this concentration of forms, the visualisations generally fall into the category of convergent thinking and represent structures. Other visualisations are possible with the careful and creative use of borders for delineation; for example, four cells (or a cluster of cells divided by a border into four squares) can readily become a 'BCG Matrix' and multiple cells can be repurposed into a 'House of Quality', 'Organisation Chart', 'Feedback Diagram' or 'Affinity Diagram' (Figure 6.2), which all extend

Excel's capability into the realm of strategy visualisation. But none of these techniques are possible with the single click of a built-in automatic function. Excel does offer add-ins that extend its visualisation range, including the ability to incorporate Visio charts such as 'Process Event Chain', 'Data Flow Diagrams', 'Flow Charts' and 'Mindmaps' (Figure 6.2). These additions (for a fee) add the means to visually represent divergent thinking and processes. Other add-ons and other tools are available. Many of these software offerings fill gaps not directly covered by a Microsoft tool or offer a different business model for the software, including online, open source, freemium and others. Software such as Tableau, Lucidcharts, diagrams.net (or draw.io) and others collectively cover all the types of techniques identified by Visual Literacy as well as variants that have found increasing popularity, such as the variant of a 'Mindmap' presented by a word cloud (Vital 2018). However, awareness and usage of these alternatives is so much less than that of the Microsoft suite that the functionality of these core office tools sets the benchmark for the popularisation of visual management techniques. As a result, a contradiction does currently exist. It is too easy to create poorly designed text-based documents in Word and yet it is still too complex to generate elegant visualisations of a variety of types or for different purposes in Excel. The contradiction is further reinforced when the preferred tool for strategic planning documentation is Word and the tool for reporting is Excel in smaller organisations or PowerBI in larger ones.

Things are further muddled when planning and reporting are both presented in meetings through PowerPoint – a tool that is thoroughly critiqued by Tufte (2006). Beyond its sub-title, 'Pitching out corrupts within', there are a range of observations made in this small book that set out the range of concerns. For example, '. . . nearly all PowerPoint slides that accompany talks have much *lower* rates of information transmission than the talk itself. Too often, the images are content-free clip art, the statistical graphs don't show data, and the test is grossly impoverished . . . *The PowerPoint slide typically shows 40 words, which is about 8 seconds of silent reading material*' (Tufte 2006, p. 15). Nearly 20 years after this statement based on an earlier version of PowerPoint, very little has changed. The conclusion that can be drawn from Tufte's comment is that for all their imperfections, taking a Word document or an Excel spreadsheet and pushing them through a PowerPoint presentation has a resultant mediating effect of conveying even less information than the original documents.

With so many symbols and techniques of visualisations to work with, the purpose is not to try them all. Developing a language within an organisational culture that consistently uses a selection with shared meaning and understanding is the goal. A desire to link up reporting and planning in a continuous feedback loop – if that is the shared desire – may even guide thinking to a still narrower sub-set of techniques. What is required is a stable system that provides an individual with enough flexibility to express themselves while still being identifiable as part of a shared system of communication. If the visual techniques being used require paragraphs of explanation and caveats, then it is not the right system (or it is not the right organisation for the techniques being used). The table of visualisation parameters (Table 6.1 and Table 6.2) may point directly to specific techniques of visualisation required for a specific need. It can act as something of a contradiction table for making a selection. But the most important parameters may be the least able to be precisely defined; is it easily edited and is it intended to be used in a permanent or temporary manner. These are both highly specific concerns that are relative to every organisation. The reality of an organisation's culture where there is heavy emphasis on structured thinking may be to discover that the starting point is not elegant but does coalesce around the ubiquity of the 2 × 2 grid as a visual device that can be created in Word or Excel and can accommodate images as well as text. The variety of ways that the grid can be used may be the basis for a wider organisational language that is built on a single consistent visualisation that can be flexibly used in a variety of different ways. As a visualisation of data in the form of 'Cartesian Coordinates', the grid is a reporting technique. As the 'BCG Matrix' or a 'Stakeholder Map' (Figure 6.2), the same technique of visualisation that is being used for strategy and becomes a planning tool. Organisational culture that is more oriented towards time-based parameters may find a similar compromise between planning and reporting with linear techniques of visualisation. 'Line Charts' for reporting in combination with 'Technology Roadmaps', 'Ishikawa Diagrams' and 'Swimlane Diagrams' may resonate more closely with prevailing internal perspectives (Figure 6.2).

The essential ingredient for achieving the effective use of visualisation within an organisation is to know the purpose and the meaning that each artefact is intended to convey back to the people who will use and engage with them.

7 Creating a learning organisation

Applying people-focused visual management

People are central to an organisation. The continuing rise of artificial intelligence (AI) and machine learning (ML) presents a fundamental existential crisis to all organisations. Assuming – and there are several assumptions required – an unlimited availability of investment capital, with the combination of sufficient, suitable and sound data, and the availability of robotic technologies (both hardware and software) any organisation could become completely automated, a scenario that could be seen as the ultimate realisation of Beer's description of the organisation as a 'black box' (Thomas and van Zwanenberg 2005). Assuming the use of existing off-the-shelf components, algorithms that throttle precisely according to stakeholder demand and a 'perfect' system that requires no maintenance, this configuration could completely remove the need for human input into the organisation. Advocating for the benefits of a visual management approach would then become irrelevant as the fully automated organisation reduces everything to an exchange of data between individual processes. Reporting would inform planning and feedback from systems would adjust actions to maximum performance (Figure 5.4). Such a scenario of the fully automated business

DOI: 10.4324/9781003304166-7

fundamentally challenges the purpose of an organisation, as the only benefi-
ciary is potentially the owner of the initial capital that initiated this combination of automated functions into action.

If the concept of organisation is to continue to retain value in an era of
total digitalisation, it is to be found in what it does for people – all the stakeholders who engage with the organisation. Process automation does have
value – although sometimes in unexpected ways with the scenario imagined previously – by enabling the organisation's people to engage in higher
value, unexpected and *ad hoc* activities rather than routine and repetitive
processes. The discussion of recognisable patterns of success in an earlier
chapter (Chapter 5) highlights the potential benefits at a strategic level, but
lower-level activities are even more prone to being highly repetitive.

This situation can be described with an analogy to the Eiffel Tower. As
a tourist it is possible to take a photograph of the Eiffel Tower from Trocadéro Square. Many websites guide tourists to this location, as it is one of
the best angles. Taking the photograph on a phone or digital camera captures the scene and it can be shared immediately. Irrespective of the time of
day or night, the scene will closely replicate many previous photographs.
If a family member or friend has not been included inside the frame of
the image, the key distinctive aspect of the image is unseen. It is not any
aspect of technology or what has been photographed but the photographer
themselves. In effect, the important context is the person taking the photograph being physically present at Trocadéro Square. Buying a postcard
(potentially printed somewhere other than France) with a better composition
would be more efficient and would not require the complexities of taking a
journey to Paris. 'Eiffel Tower as a Service' fulfils the basic requirement of
capturing an image but does not incorporate the human experience. Stepping back from this specific location, the same situation exists for the Grand
Canyon, the Sydney Opera House, the Taj Mahal and onwards. A collection
of pictures of the world's most famous landmarks can be collected without
ever stepping out of the house but a set of postcards is not equivalent to the
learning and insights that are obtained by a well-travelled individual.

These contradictions in an organisational context are the challenge
brought by AI, ML and other transformational technologies. It is possible to
bring together a series of technologies that automate regular and repeated
functions. But these technologies – especially those offered 'as a service' –
undertake these functions without organisational contexts. There is a direct
link with the way that Microsoft Word functions to process words without
any organisational context. For repetitive low-level functions, this creates
efficiency. As the functions that are being substituted by technology become
higher-level and decision-oriented, there is a risk that learning is being lost.
Alternatively, insight has now become embedded in highly structured ways

within the data of the organisation rather than as learning among its people. There is a continuum of difference that can be represented between taking a photo on a smartphone, buying a (premium priced) postcard of the Eiffel Tower from a vendor on Trocadéro Square or ordering one online. Higher-value organisational activities are those that benefit from inputs of human creativity, randomicity and even contrariness to introduce a uniqueness and personality that reflects organisational culture and ultimately its vision. The importance of human distinctiveness reinforces the value of a visual management approach. If an organisation produces planning and reporting in a way that is engaging and can be rapidly interpreted, it lets visual learners immediately connect and contribute to decision-making (Schmidtke et al. 2017). Kinesthetic learners benefit from more visual approaches as they can be guided into action more rapidly with visual instructions – as the examples of LEGO and Ikea instructions already show. The value of learning within an organisation is a key aspect of its organisational culture. It is a philosophy that is shown in another well-represented visualisation, Gibbs's Learning Cycle (1988) as well as being cited in the often-abbreviated mantra of technology startups, 'Fail Fast' but learn faster (Bean 2021). The challenge to the real crisis that AI and ML technologies bring to an organisation is the rhetorical question, 'if the people in an organisation are not learning is it still an organisation' (Silberg and Manyika 2019); with the potential nihilistic extension that when 'everything' is automated, 'If an organisation does not have an organisational culture is it still an organisation?'

Speculative thought exercises about the future use of AI in an organisation represent one extreme point of experience on a continuum of organisational practice. At the other end of this continuum, organisations that continue to use mandatory text-based training manuals as part of their efforts to induct people into their culture are a large signpost for what the new employee can expect. Creating mandatory training materials in lengthy written documents must be seen as a warning for everyone except the most focused of reading-based learners. But an organisation that sees value in mandatory training processes during staff induction would presumably want that training to be as effective as possible and to engage their employees through multiple learning styles. Mandatory training is best left for AI to complete. What new employees require is acculturation into the new organisational culture (Rubin 2014). Acculturation, itself, is best supported by visualisations and visual explanations that can be readily accessed when required to learn and to refresh – introducing a balance of visual and kinesthetic learning. A design of this type addresses the need to bridge the knowledge gap from the point when a new employee does not know what to ask because they do not know they need to ask it – this is the blind spot of the Johari Window (Luft and Ingham 1961) – to a point where they can access what they need to know at the point when they recognise what they need to know. The core of the challenge presented by this need returns to the bind of knowledge management. As a practice, knowledge management is important, but getting it right is a major challenge if the organisation is not already mature and a self-consciously aware learning organisation.

The appointment of personnel to encourage cultural change and challenge the prevailing thinking in the organisation presents a further challenge within the continuum of organisational practice. Making an appointment of this type does at least imply some management awareness regarding the importance of organisational culture. The objective for the person being brought in is to make change and to effect some acculturation on the organisational culture that they are entering. However, an observation from anthropology regarding cultural contact offers some caution regarding the process of acculturation (Stening 1979). When two cultures meet – or the representatives of two cultures – both cultures are altered by that contact. The prevailing thinking is that the dominant culture will have a greater impact on the other culture. In an organisational context, this raises the question of which is the dominant culture. When a new employee enters an organisation from the external VUCA world, this is not always self-evident. Assuming a flattened hierarchy, one person coming into a large organisation points to the culture of the latter being the dominant one. Introducing a manager or another senior pivotal role into the organisation might shift the weight of this dominance and be more likely to introduce change but is still unlikely to reach the intended scale imagined. From the perspective of synthesis within the dialectic, one culture can never simply substitute another one. Proof of this observation is regularly shown by the complexity of mergers, takeovers and acquisitions by commercial organisations when they are considered in the human dimension (Cartwright and Cooper 1994).

In this context, the importance of visual management is found within the artefacts that it creates – as the products of human action. These artefacts contribute to slow incremental and dialectical changes in the organisational culture. Over time, these actions build a visual language that is learned by the organisation, and it comes to express the culture and distinctiveness of that organisation internally and externally. Building on the discussions of recognising patterns in a previous chapter (Chapter 5), the discussion leads to investigation of the ways people link to other components of the organisational system through a visual management approach. As a nuanced distinction, the current dominant paradigm within organisations focuses on how people use digital technologies to interact with these components and with each other.

Seeing the organisation as being full of artefacts shifts understanding of the purpose and value of digital transformation. An emphasis upon learning and the value of being a learning organisation builds around the FUSY perspective. Acculturation is about providing sufficient understanding to capably function within the organisation at formal and informal levels. Sufficient understanding provides stability for the organisation and a reassuring certainty for the individual. Mandatory training could be this induction. Acculturation introduces an element of yearning – to trigger further investigation and exploration of the organisation to gain deeper understanding and become more integrated. The yearning of starters helps confirm existing norms and standards within the organisation and works closely with elements of flexibility – to take new thinking and use it. Taking a supportive and inclusive approach to the onboarding of new colleagues is not an experience found in all organisations. It might even be argued that this level of support is a defining quality of a learning organisation. Flexibility in this situation is about the extent to which the organisation is permeable to influence from a new (or any) employee with the comparisons that they can make from previous experience. The experience is a clash of culture that resolves back to the original assumptions that were built into the processes and communications and instilled in the people of the contact organisation. A learning organisation will be collectively confident in its knowledge and the evident success of its patterns. Drawing in external insight from a new colleague then becomes a balanced synthesis. Organisations that lack this maturity will attempt to flip from one big idea to the next without reflection – echoing the possession of personal (and managerial) yearning without the counterbalance of organisational stability (Figure 7.1). The yearning to see this change is done with the intent to improve the organisation, but the organisation must be stable in its message regarding what type of improvements are being sought and how these will work in their application. The purpose of the TRIZ contradiction table becomes apparent in this situation as the improvement in one factor correlates to potential diminution in another – or as some managers like to state, 'If you are going to do this, what are you going to give up?'

The ongoing balance between structural flexibility and stability is a continuous contradiction that can only be 'solved' by determining what the organisation (culture) is prepared to accept.

My own personal experience as a flexible learning developer – at what now might be seen as the earliest dawning of online learning in the late 20th century – necessarily forced a resolution to this contradiction between teacher and learner. The resolution was based on the thought experiment of what 'ultimate' flexibility would look like for a learner and what the consequences would be for the teacher. The purpose of this scenario was to then design learner-oriented, flexible learning materials. The conclusion was

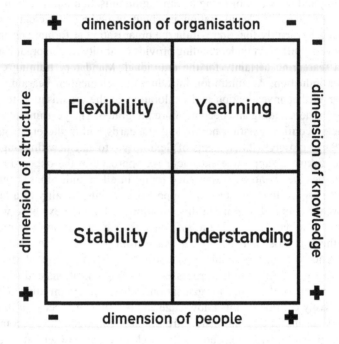

Figure 7.1 Challenges in the learning organisation

that 'ultimate flexibility' for the learner would resolve to 'ultimate structure' and stability for the teacher. Giving a learner the ability to learn anyway, at any time, would require highly regimented teaching practices and materials, including potentially the need for a form of 24-hour shifts to support learners for 'just-in-case' situations (at the time artificial intelligence and enquiry mediation through chatbots was largely still part of science fiction imagining). Any design that stepped back from ultimate learner flexibility was a compromise that offered the teacher some hope of regaining some flexibility in their own actions. These contradictions were starker in the 1990s as human ambition for the concept of flexible learning was boundless, while the technology, especially web technology, was still relatively limited in its capacity to deliver these objectives. The resultant design of pre-contact 'lecture' learning materials coupled with early evening face-to-face classes echoes the sentiments of the later 'flipped classroom' pedagogy (Akçayır and Akçayır 2018) as well as the 'hybrid learning' techniques adopted 30 years later because of the COVID-19 pandemic (Li et al. 2021). The key lesson that can be drawn from this earlier period of pedagogic development was the ease with which the development of 'online' or 'hybrid' learning materials would slip into familiar and less effective formats. With time constraints and limited development resources, the best-intentioned materials shifted rapidly from a planned rich overlapping blend of visual, auditory, kinesthetic and written materials into content primarily framed in this last format.

The most frustrating personal experience of this type was associated with the development of a hybrid delivered Java programming course with a highly dedicated academic determined to make the content highly accessible and engaging (in a topic that would be difficult to engage students). As time slipped away in the development cycle, the result was a well-illustrated traditional textbook delivered through the internal learning management system. Without the support of a traditional textbook publisher, the material was destined to reach a much smaller audience than the time that had been invested in the learning material. At the same time, the material never reached the interactive potential that the learning management system could deliver. The academic became frustrated by the lack of impact their work achieved and returned to industry soon afterwards.

There are many lessons that can be learned from this vignette. The language of the organisation did, at times, refer to the learning materials as artefacts. However, the meaning of this observation was rarely explored further during their development. One reason for this minimal critical engagement was that recognition of learning materials as artefacts tended to be confined largely to the colleagues tasked with staff development and the normalisation of flexible learning within current academic practice. Having a range of perspectives in the organisation meant that those people whose objectives were to bring change within the prevailing culture were those most likely to consider the permanence of the materials being created. There was a separate group of technical and knowledge specialists who had different objectives that were often set within more time-constrained frameworks. When faced with these pressures, the knowledge specialists – the academics – often took the approach that 'placeholder' material would bridge the immediate need and they could then subsequently return to create something more permanent. However, the reality was that this remedial action rarely happened. The default 'placeholder' content was usually text-based and sometimes was presented as a meta-description of the intended content and its hoped for visual or auditory form rather than being high-quality learning material. Subsequent analysis of the outcome of the overall project tended to focus on the naivety of short development timelines and, in some cases, even recommended replacing the visionary aspiration of flexible learning with more traditional scheduled lectures. The impetus for cultural change was lost at this point. Management recognition of the reversal in strategic objective to create a totally flexible learning campus was put down to being 'ahead of its time'. It was. If the same project had been conducted in 2020, it would have been described as a digital transformation project. The experience could be put down to the inevitable victory of culture over strategy (Engel 2018). As a form of *post hoc* rationalisation benefiting from the separation of over 20 years, the absence of much of the technology now readily available – especially mobile devices – can now be identified as a key limiting factor to the potential success of the project. The lack of smartphones, robust internet networks or stable streaming technology all pointed organisational investment towards buildings and computer labs that would now be deflected instead towards software and network infrastructure. However, the biggest challenge that was never adequately addressed was the issue of creating materials that did not default to text when the project came under pressures of time, costs or peoples' availability and skills. The learning development occurred during a period of technology development that can be paraphrased by the assumption, 'build it and they will come' (Hendrix 1999). The problem was that the technology that was being built was primarily text-based in its conceptualisation and was solely intended for producing text-based output. Within this observation, there is a return to the central challenge for visual management: to have the right tools to be able to communicate visually without the need for exotic software, third-party tools or specialist technical support.

Taking this vignette forward into the current day – with the advances in digital technology and (possibly) in management understanding – poses some key questions for current organisations. Given the widespread availability of a range of technologies, what does a learning organisation do and how does it prepare its people? As they did over 20 years ago, current digital technologies facilitate flexibility. More recent developments and increasing sophistication allow this flexibility to turn into a rhetoric regarding customisability and even personalisation of experience. These are features that a systems architect would describe as non-functional requirements (Gross and Yu 2001) because they define what it 'is' rather than what it 'does'. A systems-based approach to defining a learning organisation allows for an itemisation of these requirements. The set of '-ibilities' – as many of the nouns used for the functions share this ending – indicate which requirements are being sought out in the design of the system and – as with so many of the discussions across these chapters – set up an understanding that other non-functional requirements exist as an antithesis or contradiction to what is desired. The trajectory of recent technology development mitigates many of the most extreme contradictions, so that, for example, reliability does not need to be foregone to enable extensibility. The use of text-based formats (ironically) such as XML means that readability is maintained and even encourages other features such as maintainability, reusability and documentability. Specific technological tools that can be identified for their non-functional requirements easily enable materials to be created in ways that address multiple learning styles. The release of the Dall.E 2 generation system from OpenAI (openai.com/dall-e-2/) produces high-quality images from a simple written description, making heavily visual approaches potentially accessible to all organisations through a written or spoken description. Similarly, for auditory learners, online systems for creating (squadcast. fm), editing (app.alitu.com; descript.com) and distributing (podbean.com) podcasts are readily available for generally modest fees. However, these examples of existing consumer technology highlight one of the largest contradictions in non-functional requirements that all organisations face as their digital maturity increases. The tension between consumer technology, such as the foregoing podcasting examples, and enterprise technology embeds the greatest technology contradiction, and it resolves to a tension between the two non-functional requirements of stability vs flexibility. Enterprise technology is stable. Consumer technology is flexible.

Enterprise technology is characterised by the qualities of certainty, security, reliability and robustness. Consumer technology presents a focus on usability, customisability, experience and shareability (Jarrahi et al. 2017). The accidental and permanent deletion of a Wordle streak is an entirely different order of stress, upset and lost data than the loss of a single digital medical record for a patient. Reducing the extent of this contradiction is the challenge facing organisations seeking to transform through digitalisation of their processes and communication. Organisational governance and structure need the key non-function requirements found in enterprise technology. In contrast, organisational culture needs an experience that aligns with consumer technology (which is the technology that people experience in the 'other half' of their lives). The work–life contradiction further exemplifies the challenge of developing a visual language of management. A visual language requires stability of meaning at an organisational level but flexibility of use at the personal level. An employee should be able to communicate freely in an appropriate way without being judged about the specific meaning of the emoji they have used if the intent comes through clearly to its intended audience. It is an observation that returns to, for example, the question of generational differences within the organisation and the varying meanings that are attached to emojis by those groups (Alshenqeeti 2016).

However, technology is always a mirror of, as well as part of, its culture. Twenty years ago, and going back even earlier, there were examples of learning materials that defaulted to a more visual output. But these examples were less likely to be found within formal academia or large organisations. A consequence of this provenance is that often the mission of the material is to offer a more emancipatory form of education and to represent a challenge to orthodoxy. Orthodoxy finds favour because it supplies immediate relief to the pressures of time, people and costs – it is mainstream culture because it offers a path of least resistance (Dwyer 2020). The vivid work *User: infotechnodemo* by Lunenfeld and Gerritzen's (2005) presents a strong critique of the increasingly digitalised world of the early 2000s with pop culture colours, extensive use of symbols (many of which are now available through Unicode) and a strongly anti-establishment aesthetic that is influenced by post-punk, band art such as that of Sigue Sigue Sputnik and the work of Neville Brody. The book is a collection of mini essays, with titles such as 'Solitude Enhancement Machines', 'Urine Nation' and 'Anthropomorphometric'. The book appears to even have a second title on the back cover, User: logopromoporno. In one of the few reviews of the book titled 'Frontal Assault', Drucker (2005) observes, 'The design of User pushes it immediately into the realm of what Lunenfeld has termed 'interstitial literature' – texts to be read while waiting for some electronic device or other to connect, boot or recharge. His (partially correct) assumption that print artefacts have become a specialized subset of information technology suggests that texts should be rendered in eye-bite and sound-bite fragments as intellectual snack food.' The intellectual heritage of *User: infotechnodemo* is plainly evident. McLuhan's early provocation *The Medium is the Massage* (McLuhan and Fiore 1967) is in this book's line of ancestors alongside a cadre of European postmodernist thinkers. *Cult-ure (ideas can be dangerous)* by Hughes (2010) sets out a further critique of the digitalisation of culture. Adopting a similarly visually challenging style, the book presents a narrative of text and images that sometimes appear to be in a jumbled order. But at the same time offers observations in sound-bite styles that could act as a textbook for managers and startups, such as 'Ideas germinate in culture'. There are some key borrowings from previous commentators who have influenced Hughes, such as Toffler, with the observation that 'the illiterate of the 21st Century will not be those who cannot read and write but those who cannot learn, unlearn and relearn.'

Stepping back into a cultural period that pre-dates the Web and its aesthetics, there are other words that similarly use visual and non-linear approaches to encourage learning. James Burke found fame through his BBC series 'Connections' but his subsequent work, including an attempt to create a non-linear text of non-fiction and somewhat predictably titled *The Knowledge Web* (Burke 1999), generally fails. After the standard introduction, Burke offers the reader two pages describing how to read the book and identifies 142 separate pathways for readers to follow in a form of paper-based hypertext that jumps backwards and forwards between the linearly ordered pages. Fiction has presented a range of solutions to non-linear text, most famously through the *Choose Your Own Adventure* children's books. However, the most common format for offering alternative perspectives and viewpoints is one of the most accepted forms for creative expression – cartoons and comics. The cartoonist Gonick has created a series of educational material about history and contemporary issues, including *The Cartoon Guide to Environment* (Gonick and Outwater 1996). An even more radical offering is Nicolas Grey's cartoon version of the 19th-century radical socialist Lafarague's *The Right to be Lazy*. As an underground artist, this work is not recorded in the Library of Congress and the book itself contains no publication details – an approach that is appropriate for the ideology of the artist (Cheema n.d.) and his social media presence (facebook.com/deadnic/).

However, one of the most influential antecedents to these many examples of taking a visually focused style to learning represents an important fork in the development of this approach to alternative communications. Brand's *The Whole Earth Catalog* magazine series (e.g. Baldwin and Brand 1986) was a product of US counterculture that brought together significant imagery, including the first photograph of earth from space, sustainable living advice and resources, critical academic literature and an early enthusiasm for computing technology. A combination of sentiments that, from the distance of half a century, can appear as a random assemblage and at times almost at odds with its own ideologies. The magazines were prescient in identifying the beginnings of the climate crisis that is a result of the unfettered and wasteful consumption practices adopted in advanced economies following World War II. Given the limitations and costs of printing over 50 years ago the visual elements of the magazines were innovative and sometimes confronting. The print project led to the development of the WELL (the Whole Earth 'Lectronic Link) that is generally regarded as one of the early inspirations for the design of the World Wide Web (Aasman 2018) while its counterculture sentiments, especially the democratisation of knowledge, led to projects such as Wikipedia (Lipczynska 2005) and the Open Source Software movement (Söderberg 2008), as well as subsequent open culture movements in other sectors that were inspired by this subsequent development.

Taking these linkages to practices of visualisation, the representation of knowledge and how learning occurs leads back historically to earlier influences and meets back full circle with some of the examples already described (Chapter 2).

There are a variety of definitions for a learning organisation (Santa 2015). These definitions acknowledge tacitly or explicitly the role of organisational culture, with some reducing the purpose to an aspect of staff development but others leaving the meaning more open with a more encompassing view. The position that is being taken here views the learning organisation as one that is collectively self-aware through its people and through this self-awareness there is recognition that the management of the organisation orbits around the continuous negotiation of contradictions. These contradictions vary in scope from the largest external relationships – VUCA to organisation – down to the smallest – person to person. The contractions vary in terms of scale, from the largest challenges to the smallest (Figure 7.2). The resolution to contradictions is inevitably discovered through synthesis. A learning organisation sets out (through management action) to avoid or prevent contradictions from reoccurring by recognising the value and meaning of the synthesis developed.

How the synthesis to a previous contradiction is captured, stored and shared across the organisation is the role of knowledge management. But more explicitly visual management approaches can prove highly successful. An exemplar case is seen daily across the entire UK road network (as well as elements in other countries). The form taken by the signs is a response to the UK Government's Worboys Report in 1963 (Ministry of Transport 1963) which systematised and improved the previous system of signage. The report set in motion the design of the Transport font (www.roads.org.uk/fonts) and Motorway font by Margaret Calvert and Jock Kinneir that have

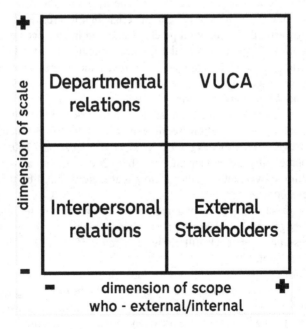

Figure 7.2 A mock-up of the Twatt street sign used for tourist collateral in Orkney

since been used across all UK roadway signage (and used in the figures of this book). Prior to the creation of this language of signage, there had been at least two different systems in use combined with a range of more local-ised solutions. The images that are used for the signs are readily accessible (www.gov.uk/guidance/traffic-sign-images) as are the design rationales for the images to ensure their clarity and ease of interpretation at high speed. Having direct access – easier now through direct Web downloads than it was in the 1970s – means that the tools for the job are available to anyone who needs an 'official' road sign. Particularly, before the availability of direct downloads, the two national UK motoring organisations, the AA and the RAC, would create signs for one-off events (but in the process each organ-isation would break the elegance of design by adding their own logos to the bottom right corner of signs). The familiarity of the language has generated its own industry with tourist destinations resorting to the form/font combi-nation for their own gift shop merchandise. Primarily famous for the juve-nile name association that it elicits, the hamlet of Twatt on Mainland Orkney has few natural or built features of note. As a result, tourists arriving at the nearby ferry terminal in Stornoway can purchase a variety of gifts based on the same Worboys theme (Figure 7.3). Creating tourist mementos may be seen as a wide divergence from the intention of the system but it does show that the language has application beyond simple signage – and there is no risk of confusion as the tourist items are stickers, magnets and cloth badges rather than being placed on UK roads.

The ability to reproduce the sign anywhere, however, again raises the Eiffel Tower problem presented in the previous chapter. The design work invested in fonts and symbols has stood the test of time as the motorway network expanded and the average speed of travel increased. In combination with the coding system for UK motorways and A-roads, it made it possible for a driver with only the most basic geographic knowledge of the UK to navigate long distances without the need for GPS devices or a cumbersome paper-based map. Users of UK government websites will be familiar with the shape and form of the Transport font lettering, as it has been used in domi-nant headlines across the websites for 10 years (Government Digital Service 2012) for the same reasons that informed its original adoption on roads.

Figure 7.3 FUSY in a learning organisation

The UK road signage system emphasises the balance that a visual language must navigate between being prescriptive or descriptive. As a system, there are eight volumes of instruction for road signage professionals (www.gov.uk/government/publications/traffic-signs-manual) which could be regarded as the reference documents for that profession. The strength of the visual language is its value and 'breaking' the rules would offer marginal, if any, additional benefits over the existing language. Using the combination of artefacts in the available resources makes the job easier in terms of the actions required and ensures compliance for the authority who ultimately pays for the work. The language embodies a wealth of learned experience drawn from over half a century that can be easily deployed and enables road signage professionals to focus on the specific context of the task at hand, including the fixtures that the sign will be attached to and ensuring that the sign is correctly aligned in relation to the road.

Many of the vignettes described here point to a change in thinking and organisational perspective. These examples point to the need for a compelling reason to encourage the change from a cultural perspective (Figure 5.3). Breaking out of the orthodoxy of current management thinking may require a breakthrough into becoming a learning organisation that utilises a visual language. But there is sufficient evidence for the tangible benefits of undertaking this initial strategic investment.

8 Maintaining the primacy of vision in a data-informed era

DOI: 10.4324/9781003304166-8

Throughout this book, the past and present of visual management has been explored with personal vignettes, key examples, and existing literature. These previous chapters have focused on the resolution of contradictions, convergence and synthesis. In contrast, this final chapter takes a contrary route by offering up three threads for a conclusion that may raise still more questions – in the finest traditions of academic literature. In some respects, the conclusions being presented are reflexive provocations. Discussions revolving around organisations, management, people, culture and technology are inevitably never neat nor precise. The three conclusions are not offered in any prioritised order and will be interpreted differently depending on how the previous chapters have been read.

The first thread in this conclusion belatedly introduces the relationship of visualisation to the wider trend for gamification. It is an intentional delay rather than an oversight, as it is a tacit alignment with the critiques of the meaning of gamification (Dymek and Zackariasson 2017) and the genuine risk that use of the concept distracts from the core value of game-like interfaces within a business environment by creating semi-trivial add-ons to existing processes. Instead, the consideration is towards businesses that have visual game-based interfaces that bring new applications and are integral to their business. The second conclusion draws on a thread regarding the future of organisations in the face of increasing digitalisation within social and business life. Pursuing the perspective of the dialectic, the argument is that no organisation can be left unchanged by the influence of each new pivotal technological transformation that becomes available. The consequence of inevitable digitalisation comes down to the ways in which existing organisational and cultural contradictions will be resolved. The third conclusion focuses on the value and use of visual (organisational) artefacts with a particular emphasis on the learning that can still be retrieved from existing artefacts and the cross-organisational opportunities that remain inaccessible because organisations do not disentangle their distinctiveness from more mundane and everyday operations and processes – a symptom, in part, of a textual primacy in their documentation of themselves as an organisation.

Games are everywhere and part of everyday experience for many as a form of recreation. Games can be seen in another way, as mirroring many of the activities and skills needed for conducting business. There is even a sense of labour (or, more correctly, grind) in many games that has led to claims of child exploitation (Parkin 2022). The parallels between business and games can be readily overlooked because 'gaming for entertainment' is so visually distant from 'working for business'. However, critiques regarding the presence of labour in games suggest that 'working for entertainment' is already a reality. The potential, then, of 'gaming for business' is a compelling opportunity and one that would significantly increase the value of visual management. 'Gaming for business' prompts some evocative lines of enquiry. The most direct example is a game-based interface that takes actions associated with the gameplay as the input for business actions and applies them to specific processes. Many different genres of games already exist, and this variety significantly extends the types of interfaces that could create input for different business functions. Thinking of this type of use can be applied directly from the *Transport Tycoon* game's interface to the operations and management of railways. Other more abstract games from the early era of consoles, particularly many developed in Japan, offer interfaces that could be readily adapted for business decision-making. The Tetris-like game, Landmaker (www.retrogamer.net/retro_games00/landmaker/) offers such an already abstract game play that it could readily inspire a game-like input interface for a variety of functions. Some developers are already thinking in terms of 'gaming for business' and finding different ways to use a more visual and engaging way to improve business productivity and efficiency for people-based functions.

The Leagues.ai system shows how it is possible to reach beyond simple gamification to produce a useful business system with a game-like interface. The goal of Leagues.ai is to produce improved performance around an organisation's own KPIs. The interface shares a close analogy with the *Football Manager* game and the purpose is similar. The system places individuals with similar KPIs into teams that are then placed into larger leagues. Performance is reported back to the system at a granular level and scoring for each team is calculated in a way that ensures comparability and hence the ability to create a dynamic league table. The approach creates competition between teams but promotes knowledge sharing between colleagues on the same team to drive their own performance improvement. By being granular with the data being used to measure performance and with the time scales for reporting activity within a league, it is possible for employees to be quickly recognised and rewarded. Being a highly configurable system means that the composition of teams can be reconfigured quickly to encourage new formations that can work with remote workers and dispersed teams. Evidence of success for this approach from Leagues. ai is positive, as the familiarity of a game-like interface combined with the appeal of introducing a form of competition into the workplace provides the types of marginal gain already successfully evidenced in the world of sport. Using the visual orientation found in current games across a range of genres can encourage creative solutions to build new ways of working. This is not a superficial addition of gamification elements; it is a more expansive and integrated application of visual management techniques. Introducing new ways of working is a challenge to existing organisational culture (it is cultural change), but, as in the case of Leagues.ai, the perceived sense of threat to the prevailing dominant culture can be softened by introducing mechanics associated with entertainment and 'friendly' competition into a professional working environment. Alongside the Leagues.ai strapline of 'Transform your business goals into Sports Leagues' is the ability to customise and configure the system to specific business needs. What is in evidence is not a complete visual language for an organisation but rather the more desirable combination of the right tools to do the job combined with the capability for individuals to express themselves in different ways – from the naming of teams to the evidence of high-level performance. There is an awareness, revealed in the system, that the developers understand the value of this type of deeper integration as a key factor for acceptance and use in the organisation – without the emergence of workarounds. This key (and recognised) challenge for the developers and businesses adopting the system is for the leagues to represent the culture of the organisation rather than that of the developers – albeit with the acknowledged inevitable presence of their influence in the design of the software (Chapter 3).

Throughout this book, organisational culture has been presented as a culture 'in its own right' to emphasise the challenges of the relationship between the organisation and the external VUCA environment. The external environment includes other organisations – whether they are competitors or collaborators – as well as the lived experience of people who work inside the organisation when they experience the other aspects of their own lifeways. Creating an exaggeration of difference moulds a particular viewpoint. An arguably fairer and far more nuanced perspective is to present organisational culture as a sub-culture of that same external VUCA environment. It is a conceit of most management theory to be blind to the fact that the lived experiences of anyone within an organisation represent only a fraction of the totality of their lived experience. This is a fact that is only further accentuated when considered over the entire life of an individual, where multiple jobs and experiences – often in parallel – are the norm for most. Beer (1988) is one notable exception. He theorised the viable system model as a series of 'matryoshka dolls' that are ultimately wrapped inside the single largest doll, which does represent that of the enveloping society.

Being a sub-culture – one of the smaller matryoshka dolls – does represent an opportunity for an organisation. Being collectively permeable and transparent as an organisation – in an era witnessing the digitalisation of everything – presents the best chances for collaboration and partnership. Finding like-minded organisations with compatible (sub-)cultures and complementary visions is potentially as simple as some well-structured web searching. The capability for rapid communication and the pivotal post-COVID acceptance of videoconferencing as a universal tool of business combined with a generally positive attitude towards openness can move an organisational partnership from concept to conclusion in a matter of days. This is an opportunity that links back to the earlier argument for organisations to purposively focus on what they do best (Chapter 3).

An analogy with the capabilities of the technology of the Application Programmer's Interface (API) is immediately evident (Chapter 4). An API is a component of code that has been created to 'plug in' to other code developed elsewhere and deliver an outcome or output without knowing how the code behind the API works. The API could be driven by sophisticated artificial intelligence, but it may be someone physically supplying the output (e.g. Amazon's Mechanical Turk – www.mturk.com). Assuming the API delivers the output before the maximum time it promises to complete its actions – according to its public documentation – the person using the API is happy. APIs provide, through public documentation of their endpoints, where the expected outputs can be accessed and the required authentication, usually a username and password. Many APIs are used by the organisation that created them and those organisations often use other APIs within their own operations. APIs epitomise Beer's (Thomas and van Zwanenberg 2005) thinking about the 'black boxes' of organisations as functional and discrete units that do not need unpacking if they perform as expected. Applied at an organisational level defining the endpoints of public and commercial services and the required authentication (including payment) makes partnering and working together a frictionless affair because of process digitalisation and the systematisation of trust within the exchange. Organisations that willingly define and advertise their required inputs in the same way would enable further wiring together of multiple black boxes (through multiple loops of output to input through different APIs) to achieve more complex desired objectives.

The comparison to architecture and its previous intellectual movements is evident in these observations. Le Corbusier's description of houses as 'machines for living' (Cohen 2004) provides a rationalisation for the concrete boxes of modernist design that were seen as a solution to the boom in demand for housing after World War II. The boxes of modernism, particularly the high-rise towers of large conurbations (Chapter 3), functionalised the worker's entire life so that they could move between the black boxes of flat, factory and public transport to meet the needs of production in the period of high capitalism. The product of extreme Modernist thinking was a dehumanising outcome that reduced people in the system to being 'just' another set of replaceable components and devalued learning (and knowledge) that deviated from a preferred and expected norm. Although not intended as an apology for this consequence, the relative permanence of architecture removes the dynamic feedback loops found, for example, within the Viable System Model.

These lines of thinking lead to the realisation that completely automated organisations are a technical possibility (Chapter 1; Nissen et al. 2017). In developing collaborations between like-minded organisations, it is the influence of knowledgeable and differentiated people within their respective (sub-)cultures that pulls back from this scenario. The desire for an organisation to collaborate with people in other organisations, and not just an organisation that provides an automated service, is at least a partial recognition of the social and cultural benefits of being a learning organisation in the broadest sense (Chapter 7).

There is a downside too. As a sub-culture, and as an organisation that is full of people, the influence of rapidly evolving, sometimes fragile consumer technologies is unstoppable. People are seduced by visually rich and compelling user interfaces, irrespective of their robustness, accuracy or completeness. There are exponentially more water cooler moments being shared right now in organisations about what the Wordle of today is than about the Microsoft Teams proposed roadmap for development. People look forward to the release of the next game in the Zelda franchise and the new capabilities that Link will possess, rather than the new functions for use in their spreadsheet. Consumer technology can be democratising in this sense, as there are forklift drivers and plasterers as well as managing directors and Members of Parliament who are equally excited by the next release of

Samsung's new Ultra phone or flatscreen television. It is their lived and most direct experience within, and of, pervasive technology-driven mainstream culture. Organisations, from the point of view of being a sub-culture, cannot deflect this force. The application of the dialectic is instructive (Figure 5.2). If this cultural force is inevitable and cultural contact is already here, what is the form of antithesis that will be presented to produce a suitable synthesis? It is an argument for the conscious use of visual management. This would be an antithesis that does not resist but embraces the enthusiasm, sometimes even excitement, for these aspects of consumer technology and meets them with an approach that creates engagement within the organisation – for the purpose and benefit of the organisation.

Visual management encourages learning within the organisation, as the artefacts elicit interest and a yearning to know more. Rather than dropping multiple dense documents into a colleague's inbox requesting comments by the end of the week, offering key visual artefacts will elicit personal interest sufficiently to encourage a further pursuit of details, relevant to their individual roles and their own relationship to the organisation.

Breaking up the artefacts of management into more palatable and readily consumable items introduces a further incentive. Statements that are smaller in scale and do not drift between strategy and tactics, recognise the difference between aspirations and previous success and avoid privileging the personal journaling activities of senior management as organisational vision. Separation of purpose within statements enables the individual artefacts that are being presented to be identified in relation to already recognised patterns of success. As an heuristic archetype recognising the relationship of specific organisational action to a pattern can guide refinement and nuance. But the recognised proximity (or otherwise) of an organisational action to a known archetypical pattern could prompt the reverse – and a conscious movement away from the intention of that pattern.

This type of contrary design decision mirrors similar actions sometimes made in art, architecture and graphics. When the artist knows the rules of design, they can set out to 'break the rules' in order to test the assumptions and thinking that rests behind this definition and in the process then discover new 'rules'. These rule-breaking actions are sometimes successful and celebrated but, often, the reverse is true. In a business context, challenging the rules for mission-critical strategic patterns is a risky approach to the creation of organisational differentiation that will face (sub-)cultural resistance. But this scale of challenge to orthodoxy may be what is needed to truly bring about the strategic change required and the only way that this will be possible is through a programme of significant cultural change. Change of this type and scale requires informed and engaged people. In contrast, tactical patterns offer the opportunity to check actions, ensure there is a consistency and define the evidence required for success. Moving closer to known patterns of success at a tactical level is preferable to a movement away. The connection to architecture and Alexander et al.'s (1977) design patterns are analogous to these observations. The 'big' architectural patterns can be 'played' with more readily to create new forms of communities and urban spatial arrangements. This form of play can be recognised in the innovations introduced through new masterplan developments. Other historical examples, such as Hartley Village and Port Sunlight, showcase the way that architecture at larger scale can be very different for the same purpose. Both developments are examples of deviations away from architectural orthodoxy based upon solely short-term financial considerations. At the smallest scale of architecture in which patterns can be applied, there are generally fewer choices available that fulfil their intention (although the design challenge still exists). For example, pattern 141 in Alexander et al. (1977), 'A Room of One's Own', leaves a designer (or amateur renovator) with a relatively small number of options. As with many discussions of patterns, the question is what is the ordered priority list of contradictions that is most valuable in terms of investing time and effort to generate a solution. Questions of this type often revolve around the contradiction of pursuing the generally smaller-scale 'quick win' against the potential wider success of a larger and more complex solution.

The resolution of contradictions is a recurrent theme in the development of more visual ways of managing an organisation. It is a theme captured in Barrington-Bush's (2013) polemic that advocates for significant – even revolutionary – change in organisations to make them more people oriented.

> The world is changing. But our twin organisational pillars of industrialism and professionalism seem unwilling to change with it. Even in so many social change organisations, where elitist, undemocratic structures are directly at odds with their missions and values, industrialism and professionalism remain strong.

Meanwhile, the growth of social media and new social movements are highlighting the shortcomings of these systems across all sectors of society, offering more effective organising approaches which are also more aligned with the values social change organisations have long espoused, but often struggled to live up to

(Barrington-Bush 2013, p. 9).

Information technology allows organisations to learn and capture patterns of success from their own actions as well as those of others. This is, invariably, a consequence of the increased ease of sharing and knowing. With improved sharing, the differences between organisations will contract conceptually at the tactical levels of processes and communications. But greater business intelligence and access to wider opportunities encourage the contradictory response at a visionary and strategic level through a need to emphasise specific differences. Differences might be expressed by an organisation in the form of its location, heightened sensitivity to individual situations, the capacity to address specific circumstances, quality parameters, price points or focus on a specific buyer persona. It is possible for ten roofing contractors to operate successfully in ten villages, but ten roofing contractors operating in one village is unsustainable. While Hotelling's (1927) model of spatial competition argues that physical clustering of similar businesses might initially seem sensible, the pressure of direct competition in the second example would force each to rapidly fill different niches and needs over a wider area of operation (such as ten villages).

The tension between increasingly similar generic processes set against increasingly specialised organisational purposes highlights and reinvigorates the importance of vision and mission. Organisational culture is shaped by, and evolves from, people engaging in immediate day-to-day actions, as well as the direction provided by vision (which itself represents the stored actions of other people). The artefacts of management emerge out of this same mixture of perspectives. These close associations should be self-evident in any organisation, but the experience of current management practice suggests that the linkage can often be weak or broken. The goals that visual management addresses are the encouragement of collective focus on organisational vision while enabling people to collectively learn, plan and succeed. These goals need to be informed by the data gathered from organisational reporting mechanisms that can directly feed back into actions. Perhaps the greatest contradiction for an organisation has been embedded in the FUSY acronym that has been presented and used throughout this book. How is an organisation to be flexible and stable simultaneously? How are yearning and understanding reconcilable among busy people? Resolving this parallel pair of contradictions would address many of the challenges

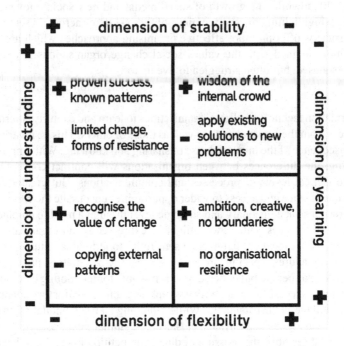

Figure 8.1 FUSY contradictions and potential positives or negatives for any organisation

found in the organisation (Figure 8.1). If addressing these issues can be done visually, then the future of a learning organisation is bright.

However, in the spirit of the argument presented throughout this book, it seems appropriate to finish in a more visual way.

TL;DR:

List of references cited

Aasman, S. (2018) "The WELL", in Warf, B. (ed) *The SAGE Encyclopedia of the Internet*, pp. 962–4, London and Thousand Oaks: SAGE Publishing.

Acemoglu, D., and Restrepo, P. (2018) "Artificial intelligence, automation, and work", in *The Economics of Artificial Intelligence: An Agenda*, pp. 197–236, Chicago: University of Chicago Press.

Ahmad, F. and Widén, G. (2018) "Knowledge sharing and language diversity in organisations: Influence of code switching and convergence", *European Journal of International Management*, 12(4), pp. 351–73, doi:10.1504/EJIM.2018.092839

Ahmed, P., Lim, K. and Zairi, M. (1999) "Measurement practice for knowledge management", *Journal of Workplace Learning*, 11(8), pp. 304–11, doi:10.1108/13665629910300478

Akçayır, G. and Akçayır, M. (2018) "The flipped classroom: A review of its advantages and challenges", *Computers and Education*, 126, pp. 334–45, doi:10.1016/j.compedu.2018.07.021

Alexander, C., Ishikawa, S., Silverstein, M., Jacobson, M., Fiksdahl-King, I. and Shlomo, A. (1977) *A Pattern Language: Towns, Buildings, Construction*, New York: Oxford University Press.

Allio, M. (2004) "Family businesses: Their virtues, vices, and strategic path", *Strategy and Leadership*, 32(4), pp. 24–33, doi:10.1108/10878570410576704

Aloisi, A. and De Stefano, V. (2022) "Essential jobs, remote work and digital surveillance: Addressing the COVID-19 pandemic panopticon", *International Labour Review*, in press, doi:10.1111/ilr.12219

Alshenqeeti, H. (2016) "Are emojis creating a new or old visual language for new generations? A socio-semiotic study", *Advances in Language and Literary Studies*, 7(6), December, https://ssrn.com/abstract=3709343

Altun, D. (2016) "Brutalism now: Rethinking brutalism in contemporary world architecture", *Arts*, 5(2), doi:10.3390/arts5020003

Anderson, C. (2010) *Constructing the Military Landscape: The Board of Ordnance Maps and Plans of Scotland, 1689–1815*, Unpublished Thesis, University of Edinburgh, https://era.ed.ac.uk/handle/1842/4598

Apte, P. and Mann, D. (2002) "Extending TRIZ to help solve non-linear problems", *TRIZCON2002*, St Louis, doi:10.1.1.527.4963

118 *List of references cited*

AQA (2022) *GCSE History: Specification at a Glance*, www.aqa.org.uk/subjects/history/gcse/history-8145/specification-at-a-glance

Bailey, S., Godbole, S., Knutson, C. and Krein, J. (2013) "A decade of Conway's law: A literature review from 2003–2012", in *2013 3rd International Workshop on Replication in Empirical Software Engineering Research*, Baltimore, MD: IEEE. pp. 1 14, doi:10.1109/RESER.2013.14

Baldwin, J. and Brand, S. (1986) *The Essential Whole Earth Catalog: Access to Tools and Ideas*, New York: Doubleday and Company.

Baran, B. and Woznyj, H. (2020) "Managing VUCA", *Organisational Dynamics*, 50(2) August, doi:10.1016/j.orgdyn.2020.100787

Barmeyer, C., Mayrhofer, U. and Würfl, K. (2019) "Informal information flows in organizations: The role of the Italian coffee break", *International Business Review*, 28(4), pp. 796–801, doi:10.1016/j.ibusrev.2019.04.001

Barr, J. (2011) *A Line in the Sand: The Anglo-French Struggle for the Middle East, 1914–1948*, New York: W. W. Norton.

Barrington-Bush, L. (2013) *Anarchists in the Boardroom*, UK, Bristol: More Like People Publishing.

Bath, J. (1981) "The raw and the cooked: The material culture of a modern supermarket", in Gould, R. and Schiffer, B. (eds) *Studies in Archaeology: Modern Material Culture*, New York: Springer, doi:10.1016/B978-0-12-293580-0.50018-4

Bean, R. (2021) *Fail Fast, Learn Faster: Lessons in Data – Driven Leadership in an Age of Disruption, Big Data, and AI*, Hoboken: Wiley.

Beer, S. (1983) "The will of the people", *The Journal of the Operational Research Society*, 34(8), pp. 797–810, doi:10.2307/2581713

Beer, S. (1988) *Brain of the Firm*, Chichester: Wiley.

Bell, F., Fletcher, G., Greenhill, A., Griffiths, M. and MacLean, R. (2013) "Making MadLab: A space for creating prototypes", *Technological Forecasting and Social Change*, 84, pp. 43–53, doi:10.1016/j.techfore.2013.09.004

Bennet, N. and Lemoine, G. (2014) "What a difference a word makes: Understanding threats to performance in a VUCA world", *Business Horizons*, 57(3), May–June, pp. 311–17, doi:10.1016/j.bushor.2014.01.001

Bergeron, F., Raymond, L. and Rivard, S. (2004) "Ideal patterns of strategic alignment and business performance", *Information and Management*, 41(8), pp. 1003–20, doi:10.1016/j.im.2003.10.004

Berinato, S. (2016) "Visualization that really works", *Harvard Business Review*, June, https://hbr.org/2016/06/visualizations-that-really-work

Berry, T. (2007) "The Manchester method as an education innovation", *Leaders We Deserve*, 22 May, https://leaderswedeserve.blog/2007/05/22/the-manchester-method-as-an-educational-innovation/

Bliss, C. (1978) *Semantography (Blissymbolics): A Simple System of 100 Logical Pictorial Symbols, Which Can Be Operated and Read Like 1+2=3 in All Languages*, Sydney: Semantography (Blissymbolics) Publications.

Boroditsky, L. (2011) "How language shapes thought", *Scientific American*, 304(2), pp. 62–5, www.jstor.org/stable/26002395

Brasseur, L. (2005) "Florence Nightingale's visual rhetoric in the rose diagrams", *Technical Communication Quarterly*, 14(2), pp. 161–82, http://doi.org/10.1207/s15427625tcq1402_3

Brownlee, J. (2012) "What are the Mac's command ⌘ and option ⌥ symbols supposed to represent?", *Cult of Mac*, www.cultofmac.com/181495/what-are-the-macs-command-%E2%8C%98-and-option-%E2%8C%A5-symbols-supposed-to-represent/

Burge, J. (2019) "Correcting the record on the first emoji set", *Emojipedia*, 8th March, https://blog.emojipedia.org/correcting-the-record-on-the-first-emoji-set/

Burke, J. (1999) *The Knowledge Web: From Electronic Agents to Stonehenge and Back – and Other Journeys Through Knowledge*, New York: Simon and Schuster.

Campbell, A. (1992) "The power of missions: Aligning strategy and culture", *Planning Review*, 20(5), pp. 10–63, doi:10.1108/eb054369

Cantamessa, M., Gatteschi, V., Perboli, G. and Rosano, M. (2018) "Startups' roads to failure", *Sustainability*, 10(7), doi:10.3390/su10072346

Cartwright, S. and Cooper, C. (1994) "The human effects of mergers and acquisitions: Introduction", *Journal of Organizational Behavior*, 1, pp. 47–62.

Carvalho, A., Sampaio, P., Rebentisch, E. and Carvalho, J. (2019) "Operational excellence, organisational culture and agility: The missing link?", *Total Quality Management and Business Excellence*, 30(13–14), pp. 1495–514, doi:10.1080/14783363.2017.1374833

Cascone, S. (2022) "A study of prehistoric painting has come to a startling conclusion: Many ancient artists were tiny children", *Artnet*, 14th March, https://news.artnet.com/art-world/children-worlds-first-artists-new-study-finds-quarter-prehistoric-spanish-hand-paintings-kids-13-2084734

Cheema, S. (n.d.) "Nicolas C grey on society's state of decay and lust for life", *Eksentrika: Arts and Culture Community*, www.eksentrika.com/nicolas-c-grey-decay-and-life/

Cohen, J. (2004) *Le Corbusier, 1887–1965: The Lyricism of Architecture in the Machine Age*, Los Angeles: Taschen.

Crabtree, E. (2022) "Ukraine health crisis: WHO warn new outbreak could become 'horseman of the apocalypse'", *The Express*, 10th March, www.express.co.uk/news/world/1578339/ukraine-world-health-organisation-warning-crisis-conflict-ont

Davenport, J. (2004) *The Mason-Dixon Line*, Philadelphia: Chelsea House Publishers.

Davies, W. (2000) "Understanding strategy", *Strategy and Leadership*, 28(5), pp. 25–30, doi:10.1108/10878570010379428

DeFrancis, J. (1984) *The Chinese Language: Fact and Fantasy*, Hawai'i: University of Hawai'i Press, www.pinyin.info/readings/texts/ideographic_myth.html

Derks, D., Bos, A. and von Grumbkow, J. (2008) "Emoticons and online message interpretation", *Social Science Computer Review*, 26(3), pp. 379–88, doi:10.1177/0894439307311611

Dreyfuss, H. (1984) *Symbol Sourcebook: An Authoritative Guide to International Graphic Symbols*, New York: Nostrand Reinhold Co.

Drucker, J. (2005) "Frontal assault – review of user: InfoTechnoDemo, Peter Lunenfeld", *Afterimage*, 33(3), pp. 51–2, www.proquest.com/docview/212118274

Dwyer, E. (2020) "Ending the mindset of taking the path of least resistance", *Vigeo Alliance*, 20th August, www.vigeoalliance.com/post/ending-the-mindset-of-taking-the-path-of-least-resistance

Dymek, M. and In Zackariasson, P. (2017) *The Business of Gamification: A Critical Analysis*, Abingdon: Routledge.

Edwards, A. (2004) *Cogwheels of the Mind: The Story of Venn Diagrams*, Baltimore: John Hopkins University Press.

Engel, J. (2018) "Why does culture 'eat strategy for breakfast'?", *Forbes*, 20th November, www.forbes.com/sites/forbescoachescouncil/2018/11/20/why-does-culture-eat-strategy-for-breakfast/?sh=3973f171e098

Espejo, R. (2014) "Cybernetics of governance: The cybersyn project 1971–1973", in Metcalf, G. (ed) *Social Systems and Design. Translational Systems Sciences*, vol. 1, Tokyo: Springer, doi:10.1007/978-4-431-54478-4_3

Fager, S. (n.d.) "Democratic design. Making great design available to everyone", *Ikea*, https://about.ikea.com/en/life-at-home/how-we-work/democratic-design

Fenton, A., Fletcher, G. and Griffiths, M. (2020) "What is digital business maturity?", in Fenton, A., Fletcher, G. and Griffiths, M. (eds) *Strategic Digital Transformation: A Results-Driven Approach*, Abingdon: Routledge.

First, R. (1970) *The Barrel of a Gun: Political Power in Africa and the Coup d'État*, London: Penguin.

Fisher, D. (2021) "Have you fallen for the myth of 'I can't draw'? Do it anyway – and reap the rewards", *The Conversation*, 27th December, https://theconversation.com/have-you-fallen-for-the-myth-of-i-cant-draw-do-it-anyway-and-reap-the-rewards-172623

Fleising, U. (2002) "The legacy of nuclear risk and the founder effect in biotechnology organizations", *Trends in Biotechnology*, 20(4), pp. 156–9, doi:10.1016/S0167-7799(01)01926-6

Fletcher, G. and Greenhill, A. (2007) "The object and the event: The power in things", in *Critical Management Studies Conference*, 11–13 July, University of Manchester, Manchester.

Fletcher, G. (2020) "Software: Video Tools Overload", in *You're on Mute!: Optimal Online Video Conferencing – in Business, Education & Media*, Goring: Bite-Sized Books.

Fletcher, G. and Griffiths, M. (2020) "Digital transformation during a lockdown", *International Journal of Information Management*, 55, December, doi:10.1016/j.ijinfomgt.2020.102185

Forrest, J. (2020) "Exploring isotype charts: 'Our two democracies at work'", *Medium*, https://medium.com/nightingale/exploring-isotype-charts-our-two-democracies-at-work-part-3-de850900ffe6

Forster, P. (1982) *The Esperanto Movement*, The Hague: De Gruyter Mouton.

Friberg, J. (1984) "Numbers and measures in the earliest written records", *Scientific American*, 250(2), pp. 110–19, www.jstor.org/stable/24969304

Gadd, K. (2002) "Altshuller father of innovation-the contradiction of TRIZ", *The TRIZ Journal*, November, http://120.55.91.217/wp-content/uploads/soft/100913/6-100913233133.pdf

Gamma, E., Helm, R., Johnson, R. and Vlissides, J. M. (1994) *Design Patterns: Elements of Reusable Object-Oriented Software*, Boston: Addison-Wesley Professional.

Garland, K. (1994) *Mr Beck's Underground Maps*, Harrow Weald: Capital Transport.

Gartner (n.d.) "Cultural change", *Gartner Glossary*, www.gartner.com/en/human-resources/glossary/cultural-change

Gatto, J. (2005) *Dumbing us Down: The Hidden Curriculum of Compulsory Education*, Gabriola Island: New Society Publishers.

Ghahramani, L., McArdle, K. and Fatorić, S. (2020) "Minority community resilience and cultural heritage preservation: A case study of the gullah geechee community", *Sustainability*, 12(6), doi:10.3390/su12062266

Gibbs, G. (1988) *Learning by Doing: A Guide to a Teaching and Learning Methods*, Oxford: Oxford Polytechnic, Further Educational Unit.

Gilbert, M. (2011) *The Routledge Atlas of British History*, Abingdon: Routledge.

Gilles Doiron, J. (2018) "Emojis: Visual communication in higher education", *PUPIL: International Journal of Teaching, Education and Learning*, 2(2), pp. 1–11, doi:10.20319/pijtel.2018.22.0111

Gnanadesikan, A. (2009) *The Writing Revolution: Cuneiform to the Internet*, Chichester and Oxford: Wiley-Blackwell.

Goldratt, E. (1984) *The Goal*, Great Barrington: North River Press.

Goldratt, E., Zimmerman, D., Motter, D. and Cox, J. (2017) *Eliyahu M. Goldratt's The Goal: A Business Graphic Novel*, Great Barrington: North River Press.

Gonick, L. and Outwater, A. (1996) *The Cartoon Guide to the Environment*, New York: Harper Perennial.

Government Digital Service (2012) "A few notes on typography", 5 July, gds.blog.gov.uk/2012/07/05/a-few-notes-on-typography/

Grabmeier, S. (2020) "BANI versus VUCA: A new acronym to describe the world", 28 July, https://stephangrabmeier.de/bani-versus-vuca/

Griffiths, M. and Fletcher, G. (2020) "How to create responsive business models", in Fenton, A., Fletcher, G. and Griffiths, M. (eds) *Strategic Digital Transformation: A Results-Driven Approach*, Abingdon: Routledge.

Gross, D. and Yu, E. (2001) "From non-functional requirements to design through patterns", *Requirements Engineering*, 6, pp. 18–36, doi:10.1007/s007660170013

Haldane, A. (1962) *New Ways Through the Glens: Highland Road, Bridge and Canal Makers of the Early 19th Century*, Newton Abbot: David & Charles.

Hall, D., James, D. and Marsden, N. (2012) "Marginal gains: Olympic lessons in high performance for organisations", *HR Bulletin: Research and Practice*, 7(2), pp. 9–13.

Haring, B. (2015) "The Sinai alphabet: Current state of research", in de Jong, R., van Gool, T. and Moors, C. (eds) *Proceedings of the Multidisciplinary Conference on the Sinai Desert 2014*, Cairo: Netherlands-Flemish Institute.

Harris, R. (2021) "Frontier and laggard firms: Will there be significant changes to the distribution of productivity post-Covid-19?", in McCann, P. and Vorley, T.

(eds) *Productivity and the Pandemic*, Cheltenham: Edward Elgar, doi:10.4337/9781800374607.00008

Harris, R. (2022) "Why inflation and slow growth, not the Ukraine war, will drive markets", *South China Morning Post*, 1 April, www.scmp.com/comment/opinion/article/3172433/why-inflation-and-slow-growth-not-ukraine-war-will-drive-markets

Hassi, L, and Laakso, M. (2011) "Design thinking in the management discourse: Defining the elements of the concept", in *18th International Product Development Management Conference, Innovate Through Design*, 5–7 June, Delft, the Netherlands.

Heinze, A., Griffiths, M., Fenton, A. and Fletcher, G. (2018) "Knowledge exchange partnership leads to digital transformation at Hydro-X Water Treatment Ltd", *Global Business and Organizational Excellence*, 37(4), May/June, pp. 6–13, doi:10.1002/joe.21819

Hendrix, P. (1999) "Build it, and they will come", *Marketing Management*, 8(4), Winter, pp. 31–5.

Hofstede, G. (2011) "Dimensionalizing cultures: The hofstede model in context", *Online Readings in Psychology and Culture*, Unit 2, http://scholarworks.gvsu.edu/orpc/vol2/iss1/8

Holzman, R. (2021) "John Snow: Anesthesiologist, epidemiologist, scientist, and hero", *Anesthesia and Analgesia*, 133(6), pp. 1642–50, doi:10.1213/ANE.0000000000005586

Hotelling, H. (1927) "Differential equations subject to error, and population estimates", *Journal of the American Statistical Association*, 22(159), pp. 283–314.

Hughes, R. (2010) *Cult-ure*, London: Fiell.

Iba, T. and Isaku, T. (2016) "A pattern language for creating pattern languages: 364 Patterns for pattern mining, writing, and symbolizing", *Proceedings of the 2016 Conference on Pattern Languages of Programs*, October, www.hillside.net/plop/2016/papers/proceedings/papers/iba-2.pdf

Ilevbare, I., Probert, D. and Phaal, R. (2013) "A review of TRIZ, and its benefits and challenges in practice", *Technovation*, 33(2–3), pp. 30–7, doi:10.1016/j.technovation.2012.11.003

Ivall, D. (1988) *Cornish Heraldry and Symbolism*, Redruth: Dyllansow Truran.

Jarrahi, M., Crowston, K., Bondar, K. and Katzy, B. (2017) "A pragmatic approach to managing enterprise IT infrastructures in the era of consumerization and individualization of IT", *International Journal of Information Management*, 37(6), pp. 566–75, doi:10.1016/j.ijinfomgt.2017.05.016

Jarrahi, M. (2018) "Artificial intelligence and the future of work: Human-AI symbiosis in organizational decision making", *Business Horizons*, 61(4), pp. 577–86, doi:10.1016/j.bushor.2018.03.007

Johnson, R. (1970) "Educational policy and social control in early victorian England", *Past & Present*, 49, pp. 96–119, www.jstor.org/stable/650209

Johnson, G. and Scholes, K. (1993) *Exploring Corporate Strategy – Text and Cases*, Hemel Hempstead: Prentice-Hall.

Jones, J., Murray, S., and Tapp, S. (2018) "Generational differences in the workplace", *The Journal of Business Diversity*, 18(2), pp. 88–97.

Katzenbach, J., Steffen, I. and Kronley, C. (2012) "Cultural change that sticks", *Harvard Business Review*, July–August, https://hbr.org/2012/07/cultural-change-that-sticks

Keats-Rohan, K. (2002) *Domesday Descendants: A Prosopography of Persons Occurring in English Documents 1066–1166: II Pipe Rolls to Cartae Baronum*, vol. 2, Woodbridge: Boydell & Brewer.

Kennedy, H., Hill, R., Aiello, G. and Allen, W. (2016) "The work that visualisation conventions do", *Information, Communication and Society*, 19(6), pp. 715–35, doi:10.1080/1369118X.2016.1153126

Koskinen, H. (2020) "Domesticating startup culture in Finland", *European Journal of Cultural and Political Sociology*, 8(2), pp. 175–96, doi:10.1080/23254823.2020.1788963

Kozak-Holland, M. and Procter, C. (2020) *Managing Transformation Projects: Tracing Lessons from the Industrial to the Digital Revolution*, Cham: Palgrave MacMillan, doi:10.1007/978-3-030-33035-4_1

Lehmann, W. (1992) *Historical Linguistics: An Introduction* (3rd ed.), Abingdon: Routledge, doi:10.4324/9780203416433

Leroi-Gourhan, A. (1982) "The Archaeology of lascaux cave", *Scientific American*, 246(6), pp. 104–13, www.jstor.org/stable/24966617

Lewis, R. III (1996) *Changing Perceptions of Heraldry in English Knightly Culture of the Twelfth and Thirteenth Centuries*, Unpublished MA Thesis, University of North Texas, www.proquest.com/docview/304268859

Li, Q., Li, Z. and Han, J. (2021) "A hybrid learning pedagogy for surmounting the challenges of the COVID-19 pandemic in the performing arts education", *Education and Information Technologies*, 26, pp. 7635–55, doi:10.1007/s10639-021-10612-1

Lima, A., Monteiro, P., Fernandes, G. and Machado, R. J. (2016) "Mapping between artefacts and portfolio processes from the PMI standard for portfolio management", in Wrycza, S. (ed) *Information Systems: Development, Research, Applications, Education*, Cham: Springer, doi:10.1007/978-3-319-46642-2_8

Lima, M. (2011) *Visual Complexity: Mapping Patterns of Information*, New York: Princeton Architectural Press.

Lipczynska, S. (2005) "Power to the people: The case for Wikipedia", *Reference Reviews*, 19(2), pp. 6–7, doi:10.1108/09504120510580028

London Transport Museum (n.d.) *The Evolution of the Roundel*, www.ltmuseum.co.uk/collections/stories/design/evolution-roundel

Luft, J. and Ingham, H. (1961) "The Johari Window: A graphic model of awareness in interpersonal relations", *Human Relations Training News*, 5(9), pp. 6–7, www.convivendo.net/wp-content/uploads/2009/05/johari-window-articolo-originale.pdf

Lunenfeld, P. and Gerritzen, M. (2005) *User: InfoTechnoDemo: Mediaworkbook*, Cambridge: MIT Press.

Macaulay, J. (1996) *Birlinn: Longships of the Hebrides*, Cambridge: White Horse Press.

MacDonald, M. and Morris, P. (2000) *The Marketing Plan: A Pictorial Guide for Managers*, Oxford: Butterworth Heinemann.

124   *List of references cited*

MacVaugh, J. and Schiavone, F. (2010) "Limits to the diffusion of innovation: A literature review and integrative model", *European Journal of Innovation Management*, 13(2), pp. 197–221, doi:10.1108/14601061011040258

Malatji, M., Von Solms, S. and Marnewick, A. (2019) "Socio-technical systems cybersecurity framework", *Information and Computer Security*, 27(2), pp. 233–72, doi:10.1108/ICS-03-2018-0031

Mandinach, E., Honey, M. and Light, D. (2006) "A theoretical framework for data-driven decision making", In *Annual Meeting of the American Educational Research Association*, April, San Francisco, CA.

Marino, C., Gini, G., Angelini, F., Vieno, A. and Spada, M. (2020) "Social norms and e-motions in problematic social media use among adolescents", *Addictive Behaviors Reports*, 20 June, doi:10.1016/j.abrep.2020.100250

Mauruya, A. (2012) "Why Lean Canvas vs Business Model Canvas?", *Lean Stack*, 27 February, https://blog.leanstack.com/why-lean-canvas-vs-business-model-canvas-af62c0f250f0

McCandless, D. (2012) *Information is Beautiful*, London: Williams Collins.

McCandless, D. (2014) *Knowledge is Beautiful*, London: Williams Collins.

McCandless, D. (2021) *Beautiful News: Positive Trends, Uplifting Stats, Creative Solutions*, London: Williams Collins.

McDonald's (n.d.) "Accelerating the arches", https://corporate.mcdonalds.com/corpmcd/our-company/who-we-are/accelerating-the-arches.html

McKendrick, J. H. and Bowden, A. (1999) "Something for everyone? An evaluation of the use of audio-visual resources in geographical learning in the UK", *Journal of Geography in Higher Education*, 23(1), pp. 9–20.

McLuhan, M. and Fiore, Q. (1967) *The Medium is the Massage*, Toronto: Random House.

Mei, Q. and Boyle, T. (2010) "Dimensions of culturally sensitive factors in the design and development of learning objects", *Journal of Interactive Media in Education*, 6(1), doi:10.5334/2010-6

Mercer, S. (1913) "The oath in cuneiform inscriptions", *Journal of the American Oriental Society*, 33, pp. 33–50, www.jstor.org/stable/592815

Miehe, R., Waltersmann, L., Sauer, A. and Bauernhansl, T. (2021) "Sustainable production and the role of digital twins – Basic reflections and perspectives", *Journal of Advanced Manufacturing and Processing*, 3(2), doi:10.1002/amp2.10078

Ministry of Transport (1963) "Report of the traffic signs committee", *The Worboys Report*, UK Government, https://commons.wikimedia.org/wiki/File:Traffic_signs;_report_of_the_committee_on_traffic_signs_for_all-purpose_roads.pdf

Money, A. (2007) "Material culture and the living room: The appropriation and use of goods in everyday life", *Journal of Consumer Culture*, 7(3), pp. 355–77, doi:10.1177/1469540507081630

Murdock, G. P. (1967) "Ethnographic atlas: A summary", *Ethnology*, 6(2), pp. 109–236.

National Literacy Trust (2020) "Children and young people's reading in 2020 before and during the COVID-19 lockdown", 31 July, https://literacytrust.org.uk/research-services/research-reports/children-and-young-peoples-reading-in-2020-before-and-during-the-covid-19-lockdown/

Neurath, O. (1937) *Basic by*, London: K. Paul, Trench, Trubner & Co., Ltd.

Neurath, M. and Kinross, R. (2009) *The Transformer: Principles of Making Isotype Charts*, London: Hyphen Press.

Nichols, L. (2020) "Addressing exclusion in organizations: Social desire paths and undocumented students attending college", *Social Problems*, 67(3), pp. 471–87, doi:10.1093/socpro/spz021

Nissen, B., Symons, K., Tallyn, E., Speed, C., Maxwell, D. and Vines, J. (2017) "New value transactions: Understanding and designing for distributed autonomous organisations", in *Proceedings of the 2017 ACM Conference Companion Publication on Designing Interactive Systems (DIS '17 Companion). Association for Computing Machinery*, New York, doi:10.1145/3064857.3064862

Noe, R. (2020) "Debunking a myth: Apple's command-key icon is not a stylized top view of a castle", *Core77*, www.core77.com/posts/97914/Debunking-a-Myth-Apples-Command-Key-Icon-is-Not-a-Stylized-Top-View-of-a-Castle

Oestigaard, T. (2004) "The world as artefact – material culture studies and archaeology", in *Material Culture and Other Things. Post-disciplinary Studies in the 21st Century. Gotarc Series C*, Gothenburg: University of Gothenburg, Department of Archaeology.

Office for Students (2021) *Projected Completion and Employment from Entrant Data (Proceed): Updated Methodology and Results*, www.officeforstudents.org. uk/publications/proceed-updated-methodology-and-results/

Oliveira, E., Oliveira, L., Cardoso, A., Mattioli, L. and Júnior, E. (2017) "Metamodel of information visualization based on Treemap", *Universal Access Information Society*, 16(4), November, pp. 903–12, doi:10.1007/s10209-016-0477-9

Osterwalder, A. and Pigneur, Y. (2013) *Business Model Generation: A Handbook for Visionaries, Game Changers, and Challengers*, Hoboken: Wiley.

Osterwalder, A., Pigneur, Y. and Bernarda, G. (2014) *Value Proposition Design: How to Create Products and Services Customers Want*, Hoboken: Wiley.

Overing, J. (1996) "1993 – Aesthetics is cross-cultural category: Against the motion", in Ingold, T. (ed) *Key Debates in Anthropology*, Abingdon: Routledge.

Owens, R. and Steinhoff, C. (1989) "Towards a theory of organisational culture", *Journal of Educational Administration*, 27(3), doi:1108/EUM0000000002462

Paine, J., Qiu, X. and Ricart-Huguet, J. (2021) "Endogenous Colonial Borders: Precolonial states and geography in the partition of Africa", *Social Science Research Network*, 28th September, doi:10.2139/ssrn.3934110

Parkin, D. (1996) "1991 – Language is the essence of culture", in Ingold, T. (ed) *Key Debates in Anthropology*, Abingdon: Routledge.

Parkin, S. (2022) "The trouble with Roblox, the video game empire built on child labour", *The Guardian*, 9 January, www.theguardian.com/games/2022/jan/09/the-trouble-with-roblox-the-video-game-empire-built-on-child-labour

Pashler, H., McDaniel, M., Rohrer, D. and Bjork, R. (2008) "Learning styles: Concepts and evidence", *Psychological Science in the Public Interest*, 9(3), pp. 105–19, doi:10.1111/j.1539-6053.2009.01038.x

Pichler, S., Kohli, C. and Granitz, N. (2021) "DITTO for Gen Z: A framework for leveraging the uniqueness of the new generation", *Business Horizons*, 64(5), pp. 599–610, doi:10.1016/j.bushor.2021.02.021

Porter, M. (1979) "How competitive forces shape strategy", *Harvard Business Review*, March, https://hbr.org/1979/03/how-competitive-forces-shape-strategy

Pryor, J. and Crossouard, B. (2010) "Challenging formative assessment: Disciplinary spaces and identities", *Assessment & Evaluation in Higher Education*, 35(3), pp. 265–76, doi:10.1080/02602930903312891

Rabina, D. (2013) "A brief history of sir isaac pitman & his legacy", *MiNYStories*, 10th December, https://minystories.wordpress.com/2013/12/10/a-brief-history-of-sir-isaac-pitman-and-his-legacy/

Rainey, A. (1975) "Notes on some proto-sinaitic inscriptions", *Israel Exploration Journal*, 25(2/3), pp. 106–16, www.jstor.org/stable/27925505

Rathje, W. (1979) "Modern material culture studies", in *Advances in Archaeological Method and Theory*, vol. 2, www.jstor.org/stable/20170141

Rendgen, S. (2019) "Historical infographics: From paris with love", 15 March, https://sandrarendgen.wordpress.com/2019/03/15/data-trails-from-paris-with-love/

Robbeets, M., Bouckaert, R. and Conte, M. (2021) "Triangulation supports agricultural spread of the Transeurasian languages", *Nature*, 599, pp. 616–21, doi:10.1038/s41586-021-04108-8

Roberts, M. (2005) *Underground Maps after Beck*, Harrow: Capital Transport Publishing.

Roberts, R., and Laramee, R. (2018) "Visualising business data: A survey", *Information*, 9(11), doi:10.3390/info9110285

Rubin, N. (2014) "You say acculturation . . . I say enculturation: Connecting employees to your culture", *Nancy Rubin: Content, Curation and Curiosity*, 9 June, https://nancy-rubin.com/2014/06/09/acculturation-onboarding-employees-into-your-organization-culture/

Rudolph, C., Rauvola, R. and Zacher, H. (2018) "Leadership and generations at work: A critical review", *The Leadership Quarterly*, 29(1), pp. 44–57, doi:10.1016/j.leaqua.2017.09.004

Russell-Jones, N. (1995) *The Management Change Pocketbook: For Those Managing Change and Those Undergoing Change, a Concise Description of the Change Process, Its Problems and the Solutions*, London: Melrose Film Productions.

Russo, D. and Duci, S. (2015) "From Altshuller's 76 standard solutions to a new set of 111 standards", *Procedia Engineering*, 131, pp. 747–56, doi:10.1016/j.proeng.2015.12.369

Feuer, A. (2010) "About this site", *Live in Greatness*, https://liveingreatness.com/about/

Rutte, H. (1991) "The philosopher Otto Neurath", in Uebel, T. E. (ed) *Rediscovering the Forgotten Vienna Circle. Boston Studies in the Philosophy of Science*, vol. 133, Dordrecht: Springer, doi:1007/978-94-011-3182-7_6

Samson, D. and Challis, D. (2002) "Patterns of business excellence", *Measuring Business Excellence*, 6(2), pp. 15–21, doi:10.1108/13683040210431428

Santa, M. (2015) "Learning organisation review – A 'good' theory perspective", *The Learning Organization*, 22(5), pp. 242–70, doi:10.1108/TLO-12-2014-0067

Saunders, M., Lewis, P. and Thornhill, A. (2015) *Research Methods for Business Students*, New York: Pearson Education.

Savransky, S. (2000) *Engineering of Creativity Introduction to TRIZ Methodology of Inventive Problem Solving*, Boca Raton: CRC Press.

Schmidtke, K., Watson, D. and Vlaev, I. (2017) "The use of control charts by lay-people and hospital decision-makers for guiding decision making", *Quarterly Journal of Experimental Psychology*, 70(7), July, pp. 1114–28, doi:10.1080/17 470218.2016.1172096

Shore, H. and Johnston, H. (2015) "Thinking about the future of our criminal past", *Law, Crime and History*, 5(1), pp. 5–11, http://hdl.handle.net/10026.1/8914

Silberg, J. and Manyika, J. (2019) "Notes from the AI frontier: Tackling bias in AI (and in humans)", *Monthly Highlights*, June, McKinsey Global Institute.

Skorka, A. (2017) "Successful dashboard implementation in practice", *International Journal of Market Research*, 59(2), doi:10.2501/IJMR-2017-017

Smith, B. K. and Blankinship, E. (2000) "Justifying imagery: Multimedia support for learning through exploration", *IBM Systems Journal*, 39(3/4), pp. 749–68.

Söderberg, J. (2008) *Hacking Capitalism: the Free and Open Source Software Movement*, Abingdon: Routledge.

Spierings, A., Kerr, D. and Houghton, L. (2017) "Issues that support the creation of ICT workarounds: Towards a theoretical understanding of feral information systems", *Information Systems Journal*, 27, pp. 775–94, doi:10.1111/ isj.12123

Sproat, R. (2016) "English among the writing systems of the world", in *The Routledge Handbook of the English Writing System*, Abingdon: Routledge.

Stamper, R. (1993) "A semiotic theory of information and information systems", in *Invited Papers for the ICL/University of Newcastle Seminar on Information*, https://ris.utwente.nl/ws/portalfiles/portal/5383733/101.pdf

Stening, B. (1979) "Problems in cross-cultural contact: A literature review", *International Journal of Intercultural Relations*, 3(3), pp. 269–313, doi:10.1016/0147-1767(79)90016-6

Szafir, D. (2018) "The good, the bad, and the biased: five ways visualizations can mislead (and how to fix them)", *ACM Interactions*, XXV(4), p. 28, https://interactions.acm.org/archive/view/july-august-2018/the-good-the-bad-and-the-biased

Thomas, R. and van Zwanenberg, N. (2005) "Stafford Beer in memoriam – 'An argument of change' three decades on", *Kybernetes. The International Journal of Systems & Cybernetics*, 34(5), pp. 637–51, doi:10.1108/03684920510595337

Tufte, E. (1983) *Visual Display of Quantitative Information*, Cheshire, CT: Graphics Press.

Tufte, E. (1990) *Envisioning Information*, Cheshire, CT: Graphics Press.

Tufte, E. (2006) *The Cognitive Style of PowerPoint: Pitching Out Corrupts Within*, Cheshire, CT: Graphics Press.

Tufte, E. (2006a) *Beautiful Evidence*, Cheshire, CT: Graphics Press.

Turnbull, S. (2012) *Samurai Heraldry*, London: Bloomsbury Publishing.

Turner, E. (1965) *The Shocking History of Advertising*, Harmondsworth: Penguin.

Unger, J. and DeFrancis, J. (1995) "Logographic and semasiographic writing systems: A critique of Sampson's classification", in Taylor, I. and Olson, D. (eds) *Scripts and Literacy. Neuropsychology and Cognition*, vol. 7, Dordrecht: Springer, doi:10.1007/978-94-011-1162-1_4

Vertesi, J. (2008) "Mind the gap: The London underground map and users' representations of urban space", *Social Studies of Science*, 38(1), pp. 7–33, doi:10.1177/0306312707084153

Vettorel, P. (2014) *English as a Lingua Franca in Wider Networking: Blogging Practices*, Boston: De Gruyter Mouton, doi:10.1515/9783110336009

Vital, A. (2018) "How to think visually", *Adioma*, 3 June, https://blog.adioma.com/how-to-think-visually-using-visual-analogies-infographic/

Wainer, H. (2003) "Visual revelations a graphical legacy of charles joseph minard: Two jewels from the past", *Chance*, 16(1), pp. 58–62, doi:10.1080/09332480.2003.10554840

Wang, Y. (2020) "When artificial intelligence meets educational leaders' data-informed decision-making: A cautionary tale", *Studies in Educational Evaluation*, 100872.

Williams, R. (2015) *Keywords: A Vocabulary of Culture and Society*, New York: Oxford University Press.

Wynn, T. (1994) "Tool and tool behaviour", in Ingold, T. (ed) *Companion Encyclopedia of Anthropology*, Abingdon: Routledge.

Young, A., Majchrzak, A. and Kane, G. (2021) "Organizing workers and machine learning tools for a less oppressive workplace", *International Journal of Information Management*, 59, doi:10.1016/j.ijinfomgt.2021.102353

Zer-Aviv, M. (2014) "Disinformation visualization: How to lie with datavis (the essay)", *Mushon*, March, http://mushon.com/blog/2014/01/31/disinformation-visualization-how-to-lie-with-datavis-the-essay/

Index

Note: Page numbers in *italics* indicates figures and page numbers in **bold** indicates tables on the corresponding page.

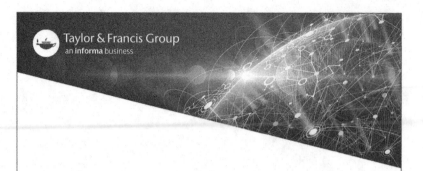